Following Robert Louis Stevenson with a Donkey

Zigging and Zagging Through the Cévennes

FOLLOWING ROBERT LOUIS STEVENSON WITH A DONKEY

Zigging and Zagging Through the Cévennes

Betty Gladstone

*Edited by
Carla X. Gladstone*

Copyright @ 2017 by Carla X. Gladstone

All rights reserved worldwide. No part of this book may be reproduced or transmitted in any form or by any means, electronic or mechanical, including photocopying, recording, or by any information storage and retrieval system, without written permission from the publisher except in the case of brief quotations embodied in critical articles and reviews.

For information about permission to reproduce selections from this book, write to Permissions, Gettier Group, LLC, 21348 Small Branch Place, Broadlands, VA 20148.

Library of Congress Control Number: 2017956253

Publisher's Cataloging-in-Publication data

Names: Gladstone, Betty, author. | Gladstone, Carla X., editor.

Title: Following Robert Louis Stevenson with a donkey : zigging and zagging through the Cévennes / Betty Gladstone ; edited by Carla X. Gladstone.
Description: Includes bibliographical references and index. | Broadlands, VA: Gettier Group, LLC, 2017.
Identifiers: ISBN 978-0-9860882-8-5 (pbk.) | 978-0-9860882-6-1 (ebook) | LCCN 2017956253
Subjects: LCSH Gladstone, Betty—Travel—France. | Stevenson, Robert Louis, 1850-1894—Travel—France—Cévennes Mountains. | Stevenson, Robert Louis, 1850-1894. Travels with a donkey in the Cevennes. | Cévennes Mountains (France)—Description and travel. | Mothers and daughters. | BISAC BIOGRAPHY & AUTOBIOGRAPHY / Personal Memoirs | TRAVEL / Europe / France | TRAVEL / Special Interest / Hikes & Walks | TRAVEL / Special Interest / Literary
Classification: LCC DC611.C424 .G6 2017 | DDC 944/.81—dc23

First Edition
10 9 8 7 6 5 4 3 2 1

Cover design and interior art by Ikumi Kayama

Printed in the United States of America
by Gettier Group, LLC (www.gettiergroup.net)

I travel not to go anywhere, but to go. I travel for travel's sake.

Robert Louis Stevenson
Travels with a Donkey in the Cévennes

Contents

Foreword xi
Chapter 1, Preparations 1
Chapter 2, Arrival 9
Chapter 3, Le Monastier-sur-Gazeille 13
Chapter 4, Humans Stride, Donkey Collapses 21
Chapter 5, Resolution to Continue 33
Chapter 6, Dutch Farmer and Donkey Repair 39
Chapter 7, Lost in the Rain 47
Chapter 8, Monastery 57
Chapter 9, Dubious Directions 65
Chapter 10, Facing the Mountains 73
Chapter 11, Path of Stone Pillars 79
Chapter 12, Tea Time 83
Chapter 13, Stopped by Gendarmes 89
Chapter 14, Journey's End 95
Chapter 15, Farewells 99
Afterword 103

Further Reading...119
Index 121
About the Author 129
If You Liked this Book 131

List of Figures

Figure 1. First sight of Modestine....................18
Figure 2. What is the matter with Modestine?!..............27
Figure 3. Deluxe restroom facility in the Cévennes—with plumbing!...........................30
Figure 4. Modestine undergoing hoof repair (farrier, Modestine, Betty, and Rombout).................43
Figure 5. Carol, Betty, Modestine, and Roberta at Hôtel des Pins 66
Figure 6. At Notre Dames de Neiges, unnamed workman, Père Emile, Roberta, Betty, Modestine, and Carol..........67
Figure 7. Map of confusion 70
Figure 8. Modestine and Carol...................96
Figure 9. Betty, Modestine, and Carol..................100
Figure 10. The plinth and its inscription 104
Figure 11. Syndicat d'Initiative 105
Figure 12. Betty, unknown dignitary, Nancy Brackett, and Dr. Ollier giving speech at dedication of monument........108

Figure 13. Betty, Nancy Brackett, and unknown dignitary at the monument. 109
Figure 14. Betty and procession after the dedication of the monument. 110
Figure 15. Jean-Pierre Vaggiani getting acquainted with his donkey 112
Figure 16. Jean-Pierre Vaggiani and his donkey reach a meeting of minds 113
Figure 17. Nancy Brackett, Dr. Ollier, and Betty at the *vin d'honneur*. 114
Figure 18. Madame Ollier, unknown man, Nancy Brackett, unknown man, Betty, and Dr. Ollier at the banquet 114
Figure 19. Press coverage of the monument dedication 115
Figure 20. Betty in Le Monastier in 1963—the picture that appeared in her French obituary 117

Foreword

I sought, but never did find, my mother's diary. What I found instead was a folder containing a stack of typewritten sheets separated into groups. It was a day-by-day narrative of thirteen days in May 1963 when my mother, sister, and I walked one hundred thirty-five miles through the mountains of southern France. This trip retraced the journey made by Robert Louis Stevenson in 1878 that became the subject of his second book, *Travels with a Donkey in the Cévennes*. Like Stevenson, we travelled with a donkey.

Travels with a Donkey in the Cévennes appeared in 1879, got favorable critical notices, and has become a minor classic of travel literature. It might have felt the shadow of literary neglect had its author not gone on to publish *Treasure Island, Kidnapped,* and *The Strange Case of Dr. Jekyll and Mr. Hyde;* but, as it happened, the book has never been out of print. My mother, Betty, read it as a teenager in the 1930s and daydreamed of going to France to walk where Stevenson had walked and see what he had seen.

In the spring of 1962, Betty was married and living in Berkeley, California, with her husband and two daughters. The older daughter, Roberta, was just seventeen years old and about to graduate from high school. I was the younger daughter, Carol (as an adult I changed my first name to Carla), eleven years old, completing the sixth grade.

As the baby of the family, I was usually informed of family decisions rather than consulted about them. My first hint that something was afoot was when close family friends were about to spend a sabbatical year in London. I overheard talk of traveling in England. The next thing I knew, we were making plans for my mother, sister, and me to spend the entire school year in Europe. The outline of our trip was vague, but one thing was certain: when spring came we would go to the Cévennes mountains to follow, as closely as possible, the exact route taken by Stevenson as recounted in his book.

My mother wrote the manuscript shortly after we returned to the United States in 1963. She didn't realize she would later live in the Cévennes. In 1965 my parents divorced and she left Berkeley for France. One of her first activities in France was offering to erect a monument to Stevenson in the town Le Monastier-sur-Gazeille, where his 1878 trip began. She lived in La Monastier for the next two years before moving to England and subsequently to Santa Fe, New Mexico, where she died in 1990. She never lost touch with her French friends.

The first part of this book is my mother's manuscript, the story of our walk in 1963. The afterword, which is compiled from letters and photo albums, describes the improbable dedication of the Stevenson monument. The monument and my mother are mentioned in *Long Walks in France* by Adam Nicholson:

> Stevenson is heard of in most places. In Le Monastier itself the name of *le grand ecrivan anglais* (occasionally amended to *ecossais* by some pedant or partisan) is spread around the town. A marble plinth given in 1967 by an American, Mrs Gladstone, marks the place where he began his journey. (The memory of Mrs Gladstone—known throughout the Cévennes simply as "Betty"—is almost as inescapable as Stevenson's itself.)

The afterword also includes an obituary of my mother from the newspaper in Le Monastier.

Time has turned my mother's story into a period piece. The Internet, geographical information systems, and mobile telephony have so transformed the world that our manner of travel in 1963 seems almost as remote as Stevenson's. I wonder at my mother's audacity in planning our trip. We had no experience in long-distance walking and no knowledge of managing a draft animal. We had a poor command of the local language. But my mother was not one to be waylaid by misgivings. What follows is her account of fulfilling her early dream.

Carla X. Gladstone
August 2017

Chapter 1

Preparations

For a long time we talked and thought about our Cévennes adventure. We had hints that plenty of good, careful planning would be advisable. Andre Chamson of L'Académie française in the introduction of the 1957 Heritage Press edition of *Travels with a Donkey* referred to the Cévennes as "one of the poorest, most solitary, most abandoned and yet most beautiful regions of France." Evidently, few things had changed during the eighty-five years since Stevenson had been there. And he had his troubles. His main problem was finding the way in those remote mountains. We knew we would need all possible kinds of assistance and luck to find our way at all but especially to be able to find Stevenson's path eighty-five years after he had been there. The most important guide would be a good map.

While visiting Paris in October in 1962, we went to a map store and found just what we were looking for. We purchased six large-scale maps, similar to the U. S. Geological Survey maps, which covered the entire area of Stevenson's story. These maps showed, in addition to elevations and type of terrain, each and every house, barn, and wayside chapel. That being done, we rolled up the maps, put them in the rear of the trunk compartment, and forgot about the whole thing.

For over seven months Roberta, Carol, and I had romped joyously through a dozen or so countries from England to Greece and back again. We had ticked off more than sixteen thousand miles in the car. We did many of the usual tourist things, but most of the time we found our own ways to explore Europe. There is no evidence that I was the only American woman who ever spent nine months driving twelve- and eighteen-year-old daughters around that continent. It just so happened, however, no one we ever met had seen that exact combination before. As a result of this, we invariably attracted attention, not to mention interest, curiosity, hospitality, and friendship everywhere we went.

In the beginning of December 1962, we were in Nîmes. While poring over the map of that area one day, we suddenly realized we were on the very edge of the Cévennes mountains. All at once we had the bright idea of driving up there and looking over some of the territory we would be hiking later on.

"No, that would be cheating; like peeking at a package before Christmas," Roberta said.

"Yes, but what about finding a donkey? We have never seen a single donkey in all of France," Carol said.

That was true.

"Maybe we had better go up there and see if we can find a donkey for sale."

And so we did.

Stevenson had spent a month in Le Monastier-sur-Gazeille before his trip. It was there he had made all his preparations. Even then donkeys were not too prevalent, and he had decided that a donkey as a beast of burden would suit him best. So now we had a legitimate excuse to go to Le Monastier. On 5 December we drove through a small part of our surprise package and arrived in Le Monastier in the middle of the afternoon. Now it must be said that we had spoken very little French until this time. In fact, very little French was all we could speak.

Catching sight of a gendarme standing in front of the gendarmerie nationale, we stopped and inquired (in French), "Does anyone around here have a donkey for sale?"

We were very serious, but he could barely get out his "*Non,*" because he was laughing so hysterically. We didn't think it was funny at all, especially if his answer was "no."

Very sedately we asked to be directed to the mayor's house. Still suffering from convulsions, he pointed straight ahead down the road. Within three minutes we were out of town and had not seen any house with a sign to indicate *le maire* (the mayor). We asked directions again, and a finger was pointed down in the direction we had just come from. A few minutes later we were leaving town at its other end and still no mayor. We found out months later that the town hall was at one end of town and the mayor's house on the other. Our French had not been clear enough to specify what we were looking for.

At last we arrived at the mayor's door and, although he wasn't home, he could be found. It wasn't long before a smiling Monsieur Convers came into his office where we were waiting and introduced himself to us. We spent a friendly but nerve-wracking hour searching our memories and the dictionary for sufficient words to complete our business there. At the end of the hour, we believed this is what the mayor had said: "You are going to take the Stevenson trip; that is very nice. You want a donkey. No, there are no donkeys here. You must see Monsieur Royer at Le Chambon-sur-Lignon; he will help you. Yes, I will write a note to him for you. You will return in May? That is very nice; we will be happy to see you again. Goodbye and good luck."

And so the next morning bright and early we set out for Le Chambon, twenty-five miles away. Finding Monsieur Royer, we showed him Monsieur Convers' note and tried to understand what was going to happen next. It was too much for us. How could anyone be expected to negotiate a delicate business transaction in a foreign language! Once again, we concluded the affair with vague impressions of what had been said.

"You want to buy a donkey. Yes, I can get a donkey for you. When do you want the donkey? Do you want the donkey delivered to Le Monastier? I will write to you; what is your address? Thank you; goodbye."

With a violent headache brought on by the extreme exertion to speak and understand everything, I left with a sigh of relief. "That's done. We hope."

On 5 February 1963, a letter from Monsieur Royer reached us in Athens.

> Madame, Suite à l'entretien que nous avons ensemble au Chambon, je viens vous faire savoir que nous pouvons vous fournir un âne pour la date que vous désirez au prix de 450 f. Transport jusqu'à Monastier compris dans le prix. Veuillez me faire sâvoir la date exacte, et dans l'attente d'une résponse, veuillez recevoir, Madame, mes salutations distinguées. M. Royer

> (Madame, As a result of the conversation we had together in Chambon, I inform you that we can supply you with a donkey on the date which you wish at the price of 450 francs ($95); transportation to Monastier included in the price. Let me know the exact date, and while waiting for an answer, accept, Madame, my distinguished greetings. M. Royer)

Without a second's delay, I sent off the following answer (in French):

> Dear M. Royer, We are very glad that you have found a donkey. At this time we don't know the exact date we will arrive at Le Monastier. I think it will be the 12th of May. In April we will give you the exact date. It will be necessary to arrive in Monastier ahead of time to have a harness made for the donkey. I hope that somebody will be able to make one. The price of 450 francs is fair; do you want us to send you the money now? Thank you very much for your help. Sincerely, Madame B. Gladstone

The price of 450 francs was not at all fair. Anyone but an American would have paid half that figure. But we were in no position to bargain. Two months passed. Then on 6 April we received the following in London:

Madame, Je m'excuse de vous répondre si tardiment. Nous avons trouvé votre âne, mais afin de pouvoir vous le garder, il faudrait que vous avez la gentillesse de me faire parvenir l'argent soit 450 f. Merci d'avance. Monsieur Jamon, bourrelier à Fay sur Lignon, Hte-Loire. C'est 15 km du Monastier et comme cela je crois que ce sera plus pratique pour vous. Veuillez me faire savoir la date à laquelle vous pensez arriver au Monastier. Veuillez recevoir mes salutations distinguées. M. Royer

(Madame, Excuse me for answering so late. We have found your donkey, but before you can have it, will you kindly send me the amount of 450 f. Thank you in advance. As for the harness for the donkey, I think it is best for you to see M. Jamon in Fay sur Lignon, Hte. Loire. That is 15 km [10 miles] from Le Monastier. That will be the most practical thing for you to do. Please let me know the date on which you think you will arrive in Le Monastier. Please accept my distinguished greetings. M. Royer)

There had never been any doubt in our minds about going ahead with this proposed excursion in the Cévennes. However, up to this time, except for these few details, we had spent very little time even thinking about our plans. This second letter from Monsieur Royer brought us up with a start. Any time we had thought about it, we had invariably designated May as the time.

"Good heavens! That's next month," we realized.

We obtained a foreign draft for 450 francs and wrote to Monsieur Royer that we would like the donkey in Le Monastier on 9 May. We were sitting around a table in our hotel looking very serious as the letter was sealed.

"We had better get going on some plans," I said.

"What do we have to do?" Roberta asked.

Our practical Carol said, "We had better get some clothes. What kind do you think we'll need?"

"Oh, yes, and sleeping bags and other equipment," Roberta added.

"Another and even more important thing to do; we must go over every inch of the route on our maps and try to figure out which way Stevenson went. I've been carrying this notebook around all year; we've had the maps for months; we can't put this job off any longer."

"Why can't we wait until we get there and see where to go?" Roberta wanted to know.

"Can't you just see us standing in the pouring rain, looking at the map, and wondering which way to go?" Carol replied.

"Yes, I guess you're right; well, let's get down to it."

And so for each of the twelve days of Stevenson's journey, we expanded his notes by specific details we found on the maps. Often we would jot down suggestions to ourselves: "Look for high tension lines; if the road really does come to an end as indicated on the map, try to go directly SSW; consider possibility of a short-cut over mountain;" etc. We spent long diligent hours with maps, protractor, and notebook hoping we were going at this the right way. Because we had never taken a trip like this before, we were just guessing that this method was the right approach to the problem.

We gave careful consideration to the matter of our clothing and equipment. We decided we could never hike the long distances each day if we had to carry packs. That was the function of the donkey anyway. Now it was obvious there would be a limit to what one donkey could carry, so we carefully compiled a list of equipment that we regarded as the bare minimum.

We found almost everything we needed in the youth hostel store in London. We couldn't provide for every contingency, but we considered most of them. Our basic walking costume would be blue jeans and T-shirt. We had already purchased excellent hiking boots in Italy. For the cold we would each have a warm sweater. For rain, we had nylon trousers and water- and windproof jackets with hoods. Our equipment included a compass, sleeping bags, plastic groundsheets, a plastic water jar, and two huge army surplus knapsacks. As soon as we had collected everything, we experimented with packing the knapsacks. The sleeping bags and groundsheets took up so much room that they formed the basis for how much extra "stuff" we could take with us. Toilet articles, changes of underwear and socks, first aid kit, camera, and art supplies all had to go with us. Somehow it looked like we could cram it all in.

Robert Louis Stevenson had suffered greatly over poor planning for leading a donkey. While we had been in Spain, the land of donkeys, we had observed carefully various means for loading these beasts of burden. We concluded that the best method consisted of two sacks of equal size and weight, one on each side of the animal and attached in the middle to the harness. For the lack of a better idea, we were now committed to this procedure.

Looking now at these two huge khaki bags, we could visualize their hanging perfectly on each side of our donkey. At this great distance from Le Monastier, we could think of nothing else to do to prepare for the coming adventure.

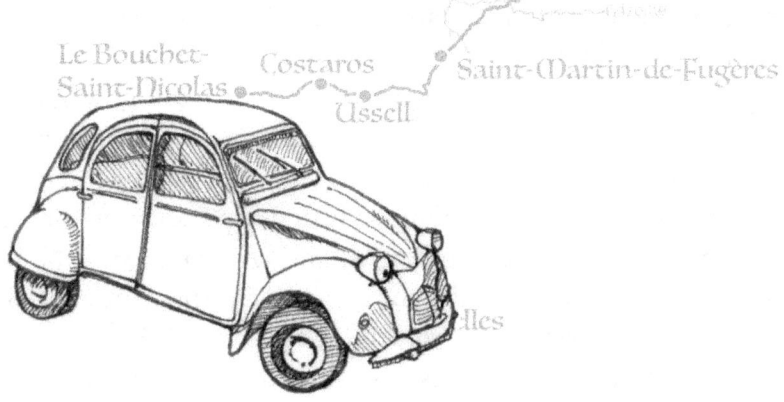

Chapter 2

Arrival

Either France is the hub of Europe or we had followed a very confused itinerary, because on Tuesday, 7 May 1963, we entered France for the seventh (and last) time that year. We had left Geneva around noon and were heading for the youth hostel in Valence where we planned to spend the night. We had to go to Valence because we knew a bakery there that made the best croissants in France.[1]

In a village somewhere between Grenoble and Valence, I spied a harness maker's shop and had a sudden inspiration. Perhaps the owner would give us some honest and objective advice on donkey harnesses if he knew we were just looking and not buying. We already knew that the price we had paid for the donkey was a special price for Americans; it would be very fine if we paid a French price for the harness.

---

1 At that time, croissants were unknown in the United States. When we "discovered" them in France, we fell for them hard and had them for breakfast at every opportunity. There was lots of variation in quality. After our first visit to Valence, we decided that they were the winners and were delighted to have an excuse to return.—Ed.

The sign over the door said Monsieur Robin, but Monsieur Robin was not in his shop when we arrived. We inquired around until we found the little old man, and we explained why we were there. He seemed to understand us, but we couldn't figure out what he was talking about. So far we had told him we weren't going to buy anything; we just wanted to know what kind of harness we needed and how much such a thing should cost. Neither Roberta nor I could catch enough words to get the drift of his answer. I expected any minute to see him shrug his shoulders in disgust and end the meeting, but he pulled a surprise maneuver. All at once he left the shop and motioned us to follow. We crossed the street and he indicated that we should get into his car. What in heaven's name was this all about? I told him to wait a second, and I went over to our car where Carol was waiting.

"We have explained what we want to know, but neither Roberta nor I can understand what he's talking about," I said. "Now he wants to take us somewhere. Wait here and we'll go to see what this is all about."

The next minute we were in the ancient Citroen 2CV car heading who knows where over a very bumpy dirt road.[2] Conversation was out of the question, so we sat quietly wondering where we were going and why. After a few miles, Monsieur Robin stopped at a farm and we piled out. At first the place appeared to be deserted, but, after Monsieur Robin shouted for a while, to our great surprise the farmer arrived, accompanied by a fully harnessed donkey.

Now we started all over again. Each time we asked a question, Monsieur Robin answered with a demonstration. This donkey was dragging a plow, and our donkey would be carrying bags, so there were some differences. We would need some of the trappings but not others, and we would have to have a *barde* (pack saddle). He estimated that the whole thing should come to not more than $30. Now I felt we would certainly have the upper hand with any harness maker who tried to put something over on us. From the looks he gave us, we added him to our list of acquaintances who had never seen American women like us before. On the other hand, Monsieur Robin was a cool

---

2   These tiny cars, resembling trash cans on wheels, were ubiquitous in France in the 1960s. They had very little power, thus their nickname *deux chevaux,* meaning "two-horsepower."—Ed.

one; he had acted all along as though this was an everyday occurrence for him. He surprised us even further by turning down the offer of a glass of wine; he accepted only our thanks, and we were grateful.

"In a little place called Le Monastier, in a pleasant highland valley fifteen miles from Le Puy, I spent about a month of fine days." Those were Robert Louis Stevenson's opening words in *Travels with a Donkey* and it was those words that led us to Le Monastier-sur-Gazeille on 8 May. We had wound and climbed through mountains from Valence on the Rhône River all morning, and we arrived at the eastern end of Le Monastier shortly after noon. The combination of the sunny day and our empty stomachs led us immediately down to the banks of the Gazeille River for lunch. For over an hour, we dawdled through bread, cheese, and wine in between wading in the river.[3]

"Imagine after all these months we're finally here; it's hard to believe," I said. "What a life!"

"We'll probably be in some place like this every day for lunch," Roberta added.

"Mommy, how many of the days on the trip will be sort of lazy days with plenty of time to paint and do nothing?" Carol asked.

"Well, three different days. Stevenson didn't set out until after two in the afternoon; those will be easy days for us. Another time he doesn't give the time, but the distance is short," I answered.

"Well, Mom, Stevenson wrote that the whole trip was about one hundred twenty miles. Now at three miles an hour; that's only forty hours of walking in twelve days. The longest days are only fifteen miles; even if we go less than three miles an hour, we should have plenty of time to sit around and do whatever we want to," Roberta estimated.

---

3   Betty and Roberta drank wine. I did not.—Ed.

We lay on our backs and looked up at the clear blue sky and dreamed of the lazy days ahead. I'm not sure what the girls were thinking about, but I was thinking of the mountains; above all I was thinking of the peace and quiet of the mountains. I knew we would be in some town or village each day, but mostly we would be all alone and it would be quiet. For all the pleasure we had received from the endless numbers of people we'd met all year, it had been a strain, due mainly to our language difficulties. I felt that a couple of weeks of silence would be most welcome. Of course, we would be friendly to whomever we ran into, but there wouldn't be much of that in these mountains. We had been told that what Stevenson found was still true; mountain people didn't care much for strangers. That was just fine with me.

Although we were not taking off from Le Monastier on 22 September as Stevenson had, we were planning to leave on a Sunday. Having already acquired the donkey, maps, clothes, and supplies, three and a half days seemed more than enough time to buy a harness, which at that time was the only missing link. Our quiet lazy days could begin right at that moment. All of a sudden we had the urge to get settled, so we could get going on this happy project immediately. We drove over to the hotel and were greeted amiably by Madame and Monsieur Rouveirol.

After having moved into our room, we went to Mayor Convers' house to pay our respects. He was not home, and Madame Convers suggested we return at nine the next morning.

We didn't do another thing of consequence all day. We wandered around town for a while, and no one paid any attention to us. This was our first day in the Cévennes mountains, and we were completely satisfied.

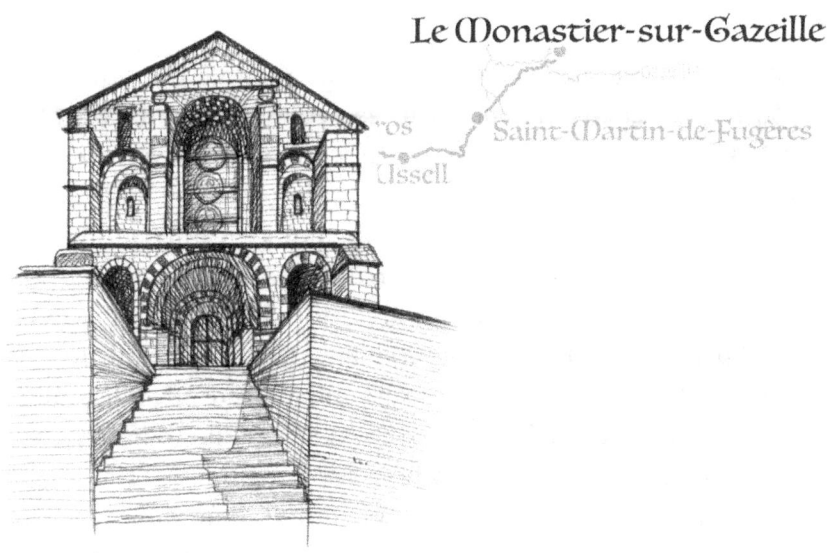

Chapter 3

Le Monastier-sur-Gazeille

Nine o'clock Thursday morning, 9 May, we showed up at the mayor's door. Our French had improved a little since we had been there in December, and we were able to communicate. After the customary exchange of greetings, I started to explain that our donkey would arrive that afternoon, and we were planning to start our trip on Sunday.

"I know that your donkey is coming today; we have been in communication with Monsieur Royer. You know your trip is very important to Le Monastier. There will be much publicity about it, and many people will be reading about our town in the newspapers."

Well, I must say such ideas had never entered our heads for a second.

Monsieur Convers continued, "There will be a special meeting of the Syndicat d'Initiative—sort of a chamber of commerce—at noon, and you are invited to attend."

"Merci, beaucoup," covered that situation and a few others. For two hours we listened to the plans. It seemed that we would be rather busier than we expected. The morning wore on and we wore out. I figured we should have a break between this meeting and the one coming up at noon, so we returned to the hotel for thirty minutes of freshening up. I could do nothing more than collapse on the bed and wonder where I would find the strength to go through with all the projected plans of the day. At 11:45 Madame Rouveirol came upstairs to announce that the mayor had arrived, and we were off and running.

The main street of Le Monastier-sur-Gazeille is narrow and almost completely lined with gray houses built almost to the edge of the street. These houses stretch for over a mile, sometimes with no room between them. At first glance they all look the same; even on closer inspection there is very little to tell one from another. Most of them are stone with a stucco plastered on the surface. All have shuttered windows. Individually, they are not handsome, but the total picture is very pleasant. We stopped in front of the door of one of these houses and were immediately received inside. The first confusing minutes were a mixture of being introduced to Doctor and Madame Ollier, our hosts, hearing and seeing half a dozen or so gentlemen who were present, and taking in the charming spectacle of that richly furnished home. The following confusing hour was a mixture of introductions, aperitifs, conversation, and more aperitifs.

Unless I have forgotten someone, there were fourteen of us present for that meeting. Three Gladstones, two Olliers (and later young Dominique and Pascal Ollier), two Convers, Madame Robert, Monsieur Chalindar, Monsieur Pierre Vaggiani, Antonin Faure, Marius Goupil, Maitre Salager, and Alphonse Bonhomme. The number of aperitifs served and consumed was not recorded.

The conversation was constant. Each member of the group took turns asking us questions and commenting on our plans. Most of them had the knack of speaking slowly and enunciating clearly, so we understood fairly well: "Where do you live in the United States? How old are Roberta and Carol? Why aren't they in school? Where have you traveled this year? How brave you are! Does your husband approve of this trip? How did you decide to take Stevenson's journey in the Cévennes? When will you leave Le Monastier for this journey? What business is your husband in? When will you return to the United States?" The questions continued.

In our turn we outlined what we had done to prepare ourselves for the next two weeks. They were very interested, especially in our maps. Madame Robert commented we could not leave town exactly the way Stevenson had because there was now no path. It was all cultivated fields that we would not be able to cross.

Madame Convers asked if we were afraid to go through the mountains alone; she would never dare to do it. Stevenson had been warned of wolves and robbers, and he carried a gun. Before leaving home I had asked my husband if he thought I should have a gun.

"Do you want to take one?" he asked me.

"No, I'm more afraid of guns than any other danger," I answered.

"Then don't take one."

I felt confident our safety consisted of the fact that there were three of us. In any case I wasn't afraid. Our friends assured us there were no more wolves in the Cévennes, and they couldn't really think of any other danger.

Madame Convers, Madame Ollier, and Madame Robert just couldn't imagine undertaking such a plan; they asked many questions about American wives in an attempt to understand how I could be contemplating doing something that they never would consider. They still don't understand.

Interspersed among the questions of our friends, we had a few ourselves: "Were there any laws for us to know about? Could we walk anywhere we pleased? Could we camp on private property? Would it be proper to knock on a farmer's door and ask him to keep the donkey overnight? Are the mountain people really afraid of strangers?"

Each question started a lively discussion among the group, and we felt we would have to play each situation by ear as it arose. "Yes," "no," and "maybe," all three were the answers to most of our questions. We explained we were going to Fay sur Lignon[1] the next day to buy

---

1 Our visit to Fay-sur-Lignon to purchase the packsaddle was uneventful. Because we had been schooled by Monsieur Robin, we knew what to ask for and got it without difficulty for an acceptable price.—Ed.

the harness and *barde* (packsaddle) for the donkey; they seemed to agree that this was the correct procedure.

Little by little it dawned on me that now all these new friends wanted to share in our plans, to be part of the whole adventure. They were now up to date and from then on would stay abreast with all future events. We had to return to the hotel for lunch, but immediately after lunch we were to go to Madame Robert's home for the next chapter. Thus, the meeting adjourned.

We were driven back to the hotel by Monsieur Convers, and he returned an hour later to drive us to Madame Robert's. Madame Robert was a teacher, secretary to the Syndicat d'Initiative, a mother, and a grandmother. She lived in a comfortable and attractive modern house, which she had built about a block off the main street. I think more than anyone else, she understood and sympathized with the difficulty we faced with the French language. Few people realized that it was hard labor to speak and understand a strange tongue. I always felt my French was improving when I talked to Madame Robert. Actually, she had the patience to use easy words and the ability to guess what I was going to say before I said it. This made visiting her less fatiguing than most of the other occasions. Roberta was beginning to pick up steam and could share the burden of conversation with me; but Carol, fortunately or unfortunately, could neither understand nor speak French.

The hour spent with Madame Robert had a pleasant calming effect on us. We were thoroughly charmed by this warm and intelligent lady. She was able to tell us many interesting stories about connections between Le Monastier and the Stevenson trip.

It is still not clear to me how many people have followed in the route of the adventurous Scotsman. The most famous is Vera Singer. In 1949 this twenty-three-year-old English girl made the whole trip alone with a donkey. The Syndicat d'Initiative of Le Puy-en-Velay arranged her trip in advance. She was expected by each town all along the way. During our trip many people told us their memories of Mademoiselle Singer. She created a real sensation.

In 1956 Mr. J. L. White, an Australian, also completed the trip alone with a donkey. In 1957 two British journalists, Shirley Williamson, age twenty-two, and John Harrison, age twenty-seven, followed the route also with a donkey. As far as I know, those were the only ones who walked the whole way and took a donkey with them. Some people have tried to do it on horseback and one group on motorcycles. The only other American to do it was a woman from New England on a horse.

Before we left Madame Robert's home, she pointed out the road across the valley that we would follow after we left Le Monastier. She promised to follow us with binoculars as far as she could and said she would wave to us with a large white cloth.

Le Monastier has two major claims to fame. The first is that it's the starting point of Robert Louis Stevenson's trip. The second is the eleventh-century church, which was part of the monastery that dates back to the seventh century and that explains the name of the town. Although few people go to Le Monastier to begin the famous journey through the Cévennes mountains, many come to see the beautiful old church. Accordingly, we went with Madame Robert at three o'clock to keep an appointment with the Abbé to visit the church and see its treasures.

During this solemn and dignified hour, the great front door suddenly flew open, and Doctor Ollier burst in shouting, *"Modestine est ici!"* ("Modestine is here!").

The frustration of the language barrier once more hit us. How could we politely tell this dedicated Abbé that we were honored by the opportunity to visit him and this great historical site, but we couldn't wait one second to see our donkey? With her usual kindness and understanding, Madame Robert accurately assessed our problem. The Abbé was told by Madame Robert that for the moment the donkey must take precedence over the church; we muttered hasty thank-yous and farewells and raced out of the church.

Down the hill we ran to the main street. Here we found a 2CV, the smallest of all Citroen cars, parked right in the middle of town. In the back seat was the smallest of all donkeys, our Modestine.

Monsieur Royer and his brother had brought her; and, as soon as we appeared, they unfolded her from the car. The poor baby was shaking from the ordeal of the trip and didn't seem happy to see us.

Figure 1. First sight of Modestine

We, on the other hand, were delighted to make her acquaintance. Up to that moment, we had no idea of what she would look like. We had always hoped that she would be as close to the description of the original Modestine as possible. Now we knew she was all but a carbon copy. First, she was a she, and the name *Modestine* would be appropriate. Second, she was "not much bigger than a dog, the color of a mouse, with a kindly eye and determined under-jaw," Stevenson's exact words.

We disliked leaving her so soon, but we had to return to the church to finish our visit. It had been arranged that Monsieur Ernest Charre would let Modestine share his barn with the cows; it was here we installed her.

Going back to the church, we could not find the Abbé; I guess he thought we wouldn't be back. Madame Robert left us at that point. Carol ran back to the hotel to get the lead rope we had purchased earlier and then met us minutes later at Monsieur Charre's barn. We attached the lead rope and led her out into the street.

This was a moment of deep significance to us. We had acquired a new member of the family, and we were most anxious to try her out. She was the vital key to the success of our forthcoming adventure. We were not going to demand very much of her. The packs would weigh no more than fifty pounds in total. All she had to do was move. We expected that we might have to learn some technique to ensure her moving on demand.

Stevenson suffered greatly in the early stages of his trip when his Modestine alternated between walking too slow and stopping altogether. Beating her with a stick improved the situation as long as the beating continued, but he wore himself out with this method very quickly. It wasn't until some helpful soul provided him with a sharp pin stuck into a stick that the problem was solved. Carol and Roberta were definite on the subject: no pins for our donkey. I kept the pin in mind as a last resort, but hoped it would never come to that.

We led Modestine out of Monsieur Charre's barn very easily. She walked sedately down the little street. We were relieved that she was behaving, because every shuttered window on the street was open and full of people watching the promenade. At the corner we turned to go down a steep, narrow path. About ten paces along, Modestine stopped. We talked to her; we coaxed her; we pulled the rope. She had taken root on the spot and didn't seem to care one bit about the embarrassment we suffered in front of so many people.

Naturally, everyone shouted bits of advice, and someone handed us a stick. The girls cried "No, don't hit her!" while I was torn between hitting and not hitting her. I was certainly influenced in my dilemma by the presence of the crowd. I would be a coward in the eyes of some if I hit that little animal, but I would be a coward to all the others for failing to bend that beast's will to my own. After about ten minutes of this embarrassing public spectacle, I was ready to try anything. Timidly, I brushed Modestine's hindquarter with the stick. The girls cried that I was mean and the crowd yelled, "Harder!" I did hit harder, the stick broke, but Modestine very slowly started to move. By the time we arrived at the main street, everybody in town was either hanging out of a window or in the street. We beamed at everybody proudly while we continued to lead Modestine along.

A few steps down the street was a café, which belonged to Monsieur Chalindar. The doorway was choked with all the members of the Syndicat d'Initiative, the two Royers, and various others. They invited me in to help them celebrate this fine hour, and so I left the girls to continue through the rest of town and back to Monsieur Charre's.

Inside the champagne began to flow, and the day reached its all-time high. Everyone was talking and laughing at once. Six hours before I hadn't met most of these people, and now we were all joking and kidding each other at a mad rate. Poor Monsieur Royer was the butt of many of the jokes.

"He's a thief; he robbed you!"

There was no doubt in anyone's mind that 450 francs was a very fancy price to pay for a donkey.

"Your car was too small to transport that poor animal!"

"You should be sent to prison!"

This was all very good-natured and Monsieur Royer took it very well. Then it was my turn.

"You must buy silver shoes for the donkey!"

Very seriously I answered, "I should!" because I had missed the word silver and thought I was being advised to get the donkey shod. This gave them all an opportunity to laugh at my expense until I understood what they had said.

Monsieur Charre, Modestine's host, was in our group, and I was warned: "You shouldn't leave Modestine with Monsieur Charre; he will steal her!"

I was given all kinds of advice, and it was probably just as well I didn't understand it all.

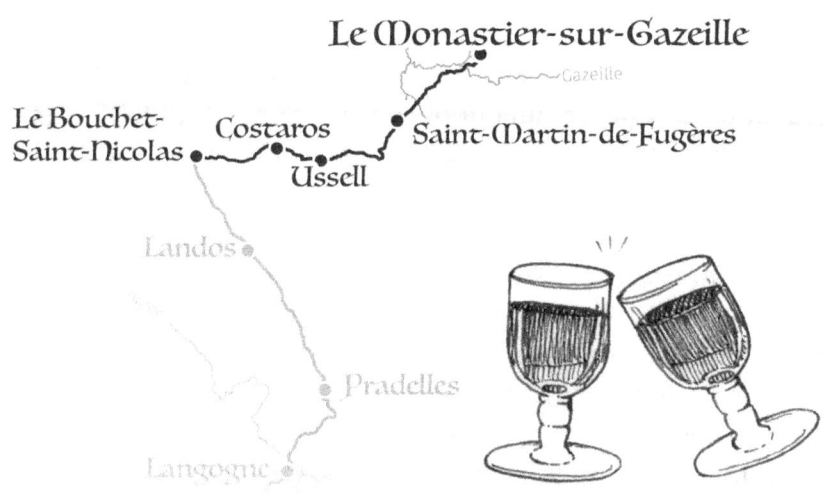

CHAPTER 4

Humans Stride, Donkey Collapses

We were launched. On Sunday, 12 May, with the last *au revoirs* fading behind us, we were almost ashamed of how happy we were to be alone. The past four days, no matter how much fun, had been a constant strain because of the language problem. Here at last was the moment we had been preparing and waiting for. The day was perfect; clear, sunny, and warm. Our clothes were comfortable. We were in perfect health. Our packs hung well on each side of the little pack saddle. Modestine was a model pack animal. She was walking very slowly, but we had only sixteen miles to go. If her rate was three miles an hour, we figured we could reach our destination, Le Bouchet-Saint-Nicolas, in a little over five hours of walking.

The contrast with the excitement during our days in Le Monastier-sur-Gazeille made the prospect of long hours on the road seem a bit dull. That was all right with us; we could use a bit of boredom for a while. During the previous eight months we had been traveling together, we had never run out of conversation. We didn't expect to now. We chatted about the realization of our dream; twelve peaceful days walking through the Cévennes.

Because of cultivated fields, we had not been able to follow a straight southeastern course out of town. Instead, we had to stay on the road that described a huge *U;* the first side of the *U* led us down to the Gazeille River and the other side uphill away from the river. When we were directly across the little valley from Le Monastier, we arrived at the tiny village of Sainte-Victoire. We were astonished to find every man, woman, and child out in the street waiting for us to walk by. It never occurred to us that the item in the newspaper would be read with interest by anyone who didn't know us. We were delighted with the pleasant curiosity about Modestine.

Questions were asked one after another.

"How old is the donkey?"

"What's her name?"

"Where did you buy her?"[1]

Of course, everyone had to examine Modestine's teeth to make certain she was four years old. We felt like proud parents with an exceptional child. After fifteen minutes of conversation, we realized we could spend the rest of the day there if we didn't take the initiative to leave. Amid a chorus of *au revoir* and *bon voyage* we continued down the road.

"Imagine all those people wanting to see us and talk to us!"

We thought it was very friendly of them. A little further on we saw a group of children on a hill. When they saw us, they started to wave madly and laugh. We laughed and waved back as they disappeared around a bend in the road. As we rounded the bend, there was Saint-Martin-de-Fugères. The children, who we now realized had been looking for us, had spread the news in the village. Once more, every single inhabitant crowded down on the road to talk to us; again, the great curiosity about Modestine and the friendliness of the people.

---

1 We were asked these same questions so many times that among ourselves we started calling them "The Questions."—Ed.

Suddenly, we thought about all the little villages between here and Bouchet, and we very quickly decided we had better ration our time. If this kind of thing continued all day, we could never reach Bouchet by nightfall. We certainly didn't want these people who had looked forward to meeting us to be disappointed. We just had to figure out a diplomatic way to please them but to keep moving, too.

Poor Carol had had enough French to last her for quite a while. Modestine, who was the center of attraction, didn't care one way or another about all the fuss she had stirred up. We were beginning to suspect that her gait was something less than three miles an hour. To satisfy everyone concerned, we worked out the following system. We could all stop for a few minutes to say *bon jour* to anyone who cared to talk to us. Then Roberta and I could wait a little longer until all the questions were answered.

Carol in the meantime would be relieved of the strain of conversation and could get a little head start with the pokey donkey. With all the months we had to plan for this trip, we had never contemplated this situation.

Just past Saint-Martin-de-Fugères, we were attracted by a voice calling from a meadow. We were startled to see a little old lady dressed in black, running like mad and shouting to us. Of course, we stopped to see what she wanted. We helped her up an embankment and under a barbed wire fence and waited until she caught her breath.

"Would you care to come to my home for some wine or some coffee?" she asked.

How could we refuse? Well, it wasn't easy. We are not tough by nature, but, knowing how much of this kind of thing to anticipate, we decided to decline.

"Thank you so much for inviting us, but we have many miles to go before we reach Bouchet."

She was so awed we planned to walk all the way to Bouchet that day that she understood that, of course, we must go on.

Now we really had something to talk about. The stopping and starting and the effort to converse had begun to tire us. We could afford no more delays, and we had to conserve our energy. How? As we were pondering the answer, a car came along and stopped. It was Monsieur Convers. He had not been in the farewell party at Le Monastier because he was partaking in the annual Victory in Europe (VE) Day ceremony in church. Now he invited us to take an aperitif with him when we arrived at Goudet. His children, Roland and Françoise, were with him, and we invited them to walk the rest of the way with us. This was not a good way to conserve our energy. If our French had been better, maybe it wouldn't have been so difficult to walk and talk at the same time.

The children were thrilled to be allowed to walk along with us. They took turns leading Modestine, and I'm certain they felt honored. Roland, about ten years old, was infatuated with Roberta, and presented her with a couple of trinkets.

By noon we started the long downhill grade into Goudet. What an exciting panorama! The typically French gray stone houses all clustered together in a tiny valley.

Steep mountain walls rose from all sides; and the Loire River, just a few miles from its source, was a sparkling brook through the center of the village. We recognized the ruin of the ancient Château de Beaufort (Beaufort Castle) from Stevenson's description. This was the first of many landmarks that Stevenson's book provided for us. They were always happy reminders that we were accomplishing what we had set out to do: to follow his course. Later on, in less well-marked areas, we found them most reassuring.

We arrived at the hotel in Goudet shortly after noon. We were determined to have a quick lunch and leave within the hour, because in three hours we had covered less than half the distance to Bouchet. Our determination flew out the window very quickly; we spent three hours in Goudet! Monsieur Convers had rounded up the mayor of Goudet and a couple of other local lights. Immediately, we embarked on a preluncheon round of aperitifs replete with toasts and expressions of good will.

The proprietor of the hotel, Monsieur Senac, was the grandson of Stevenson's host. He was in a high state of excitement having us there and sent his wife off to hunt for the famous photograph that Stevenson had admired. It was found and history was repeated as the newest crop of travelers with a donkey examined a previous Monsieur Senac who was "Professor of Fencing and Champion of the two Americas."[2]

Being very new at the art of diplomacy, it was difficult to know at exactly which moment it would be polite to leave the gentlemen and go into the dining room. I hinted that we were hungry.

"Have another drink!" was the answer.

I sent the children into the dining room to order; I thought that would save time and also maybe our friends would get the point. In the end I had to be firm. A car can drive from Le Monastier to Bouchet in half an hour. I'm certain none of these fine gentlemen could visualize what a long, slow journey it is on foot.

The impasse of the cocktail hour having been overcome, we now fell into a new one. The dining room was full of people. It was obvious from the stares that everyone was talking about us. Instead of eating, they took turns going to the window to look at Modestine, who was tied to a tree by the Loire. Fortunately, only a few of these folks were curious enough to talk to us. A group of children who were studying English occupied most of our dinner time.

In spite of our comfortable, well-fitting hiking boots, our feet had developed a few sore spots. Being stalwarts, we hated to admit our weakness to anyone. With the numerous people who kept flocking around us, it was hard to find a solitary moment and place to remove our boots and repair damages. We did at last accomplish this, and the last obstacle to our departure was removed. It was now three o'clock, and we prayed we could continue for the rest of the afternoon without any further delays. It was very hot and the road very steep as we climbed out of the little valley. We were extremely ashamed of ourselves over our attitude toward our many well-wishers. Of course, we were touched beyond measure by all the attention. There was no

---

[2] Stevenson wrote: "... here in the inn you may find an engraved portrait of the host's nephew, Régis Senac, "Professor of Fencing and Champion of the Two Americas" a distinction gained by him, along with the sum of five hundred dollars, at Tamany Hall, New York, on the 10th April 1876." I was curious to learn more about Régis Senac and searched the Internet, finding photos of him and his son Louis, also a fencer, and references to their treatise, *The Art of Fencing*, published in 1904. The book is still available for sale.—Ed.

question about that. But we discovered at this early stage that walking up and down the mountains for many miles a day would be very, very difficult for us. We had expected the first day, which would be one of the longest days, to be a problem because our muscles weren't used to such a workout. Already we were tired and aching, and we had sore feet. The strain of being polite and smiling under these conditions was pretty tough.

Oddly enough, our morale was high. We laughed and joked. We made fun of Robert Louis Stevenson because he had had different, but worse, problems than we had on the first day. At Ville d'Ussel, his top-heavy pack had given up the ghost and collapsed in the dust. We were darned pleased with ourselves for avoiding that kind of pitfall.

Also, our Modestine had marched right along not giving us the constant grief the original one had. While we were roaring with laughter about how clever we were, calamity struck! With absolutely no warning, Modestine collapsed in the middle of the road!

We were stunned by the suddenness of the tragedy. It was minutes before we could think of anything. Our first reaction was one of complete frustration. We couldn't think of one thing to do. Not having any idea what ailed the beast, we couldn't anticipate what the next move should be. For the lack of anything else to do, we examined Modestine carefully. For all we knew she was dying. She lay half on her side with her head stretched out on the road. As soon as we could start to think, we decided we had better try to unload the packs. This wasn't too easy because of the way she had fallen. To add to our woes, we broke a strap on the saddle trying to pull it off the donkey, who was lying with her weight on it.

While we were tugging away at the packs and the saddle, a car drove by and stopped. Three men jumped out. We told them our story, hoping that by magic one of them could restore Modestine to her former healthy state. Their only contribution, alas, was to haul that hunk of animal flesh to the side of the road.

We were in a complete quandary as to what to do. The men were going to the next town, Costoras, and offered a ride. We couldn't go off and leave Modestine lying by the road, but neither could we accomplish anything by standing there and looking at her. Finally,

Figure 2. What is the matter with Modestine?!

Roberta and the packs were driven off to Costoras. Perhaps she could find someone to help us or, all else failing, could telephone someone in Le Monastier. Carol and I waited, but not for long. No sooner had the car driven off than Modestine decided not to die and stood up and started to munch grass as if nothing had ever happened.

We immediately started off for Costoras. Of course, we were somewhat relieved; but, not knowing what had caused the catastrophe, we suspected it might be repeated. We just didn't know. In Costoras, Roberta had no luck in either finding help or reaching a friend on the telephone.

It had been very hot, and we thought that perhaps Modestine needed water. She had refused to drink at noon and once again she stubbornly backed off from the pail of water we offered to her. So much for that theory. Well, at least she was standing up, so we decided to reload her and see what would happen. We no sooner got underway when we saw a herd of long-horned cows coming down the road toward us. When the cows spotted Modestine, they started to close in on us. We didn't think anything of this until we realized that they were almost upon us and still coming.

We were scared stiff. I can't imagine what the farmer was thinking, because it wasn't until the last second that he shouted to his dog and the dog turned the herd in another direction.

The day had by now taken the form of an obstacle course, and we had had just about enough. We ached from head to foot. We had so many things to worry about; we were crestfallen. Our main worry was Modestine, since she was the key to our whole trip. We discussed the possibility of dividing the load and carrying it on our backs. This was really out of the question, and we knew it. We assumed that Modestine would not be able to complete the trip. Even if she could, we wondered whether we could.

This was a black hour for us, and it didn't become brighter as Modestine collapsed for the second time. We couldn't find a thing to say as we patiently unloaded her and waited to see what would happen. Once again, she finally stood; once again, we reloaded her and plodded on. Every last vestige of a sense of humor vanished with the third collapse; in fact, we became very grim. At this point it was almost eight p.m., and we had just about reached our destination. Although we had sympathy for Modestine, who was obviously suffering from something, we felt a little vicious, too. With Roberta tugging at the tow rope, I went behind and delivered a sharp blow with a stick. That did it. Off we went again, and the next thing we knew we arrived in Bouchet.

It had been a long, difficult eleven hours since we took our first step of the journey. Now what we needed was a magic wand to clear away all the obstacles that prevented us from falling into bed immediately. We couldn't walk another step. We couldn't say another word to anybody—except that we did. During the months of daydreaming about this charming excursion, evenings were always delightful. Modestine would be tucked away in some farmer's barn, and we would savor the charm of a delicious French dinner in a pleasant French inn. Alas, the daydream and the realization had discrepancies up and down the line.

Quite a crowd of people had gathered around to satisfy their curiosity about us.

Mustering up the last ounce of breath, I asked (in French, of course), "Is there a farmer near here who can keep our donkey for the night?"

We were standing in front of a very dilapidated building that was marked *Hôtel*. Luckily, the next door neighbor had room in his barn and was willing to take care of our baby. That done, we had to see about arrangements for ourselves. Monsieur Convers had asked us to be sure to pay our respects to the mayor of Bouchet and we felt obligated to do so. Before we tackled that one, however, we entered the hotel to see what the situation was.

Instinctively, we felt it wasn't going to be just a simple matter of registering, eating dinner, and going to bed. There was something most unhotelly about the place.

"Do you have a room for three?" we asked tentatively.

While the answer was yes, Madame looked very startled and continued to explain she would have to prepare the rooms.

Then we broached the subject of dinner.

Madame looked even more worried and asked us what we would like. We were probably the first guests they had had in ages, and they were in a fit of anxiety about what to do about us. We tried to calm the poor lady down and told her that anything she could do would be much appreciated, but it had no effect. She started running around in all directions at once, making arrangements about the rooms and the dinner. We thought it best to leave her alone and go around to see the mayor.

We had a pleasant visit with His Honor, an aperitif, and friendly conversation. After a short while, pleading exhaustion (which was the understatement of the day), we returned to the hotel to eat dinner. The meal was not good; in fact, it was very bad, but we were too tired to care.

Figure 3. Deluxe restroom facility in the Cévennes—with plumbing!

Monsieur finally showed us upstairs to our rooms by a flight of stairs inside the house. When we reached the top, Madame came running out shouting, *"Non, non,"* and we had to descend and go up again by a flight of stairs on the outside of the building. We could never figure that one out.

We had two rooms. They were very bare with unpainted floors and walls. There was an absolute minimum of furniture; no running water, just a pitcher of cold water and a bowl. But the sheets on the bed were the most handsome I had ever seen: snowy white, embroidered, and trimmed with lace! This is not uncommon in Europe, and we had encountered this phenomenon before in the homes of poor people in Spain, Germany, and other parts of France.

Now we almost had it made. One more thing and we could retire. Where was it? It's difficult to describe the route we had to take without drawing a floorplan. It was on our floor. It was just a hole in the floor; no water, of course. And at last we could go to sleep. In fact, by that time we couldn't have possibly done anything else.

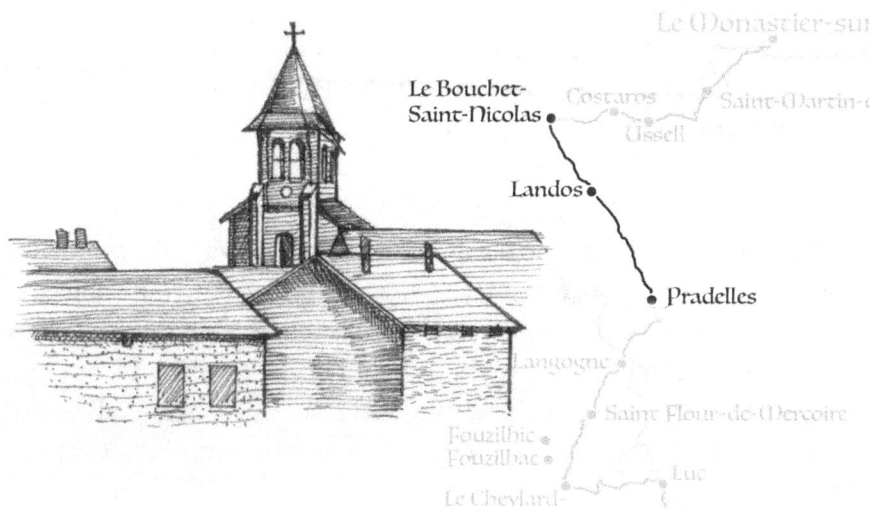

CHAPTER 5

Resolution to Continue

We had packed a bushel full of events during the long, sixteen-hour first day on the road. We were not the same smiling girls at bedtime that we were at daybreak on Sunday. Twenty-four hours later, Monday, 13 May, here was the picture: We were rested. We had no thoughts about giving up the trip. But we ached, our feet were sore, and heaven only knew what Modestine's plans for the day were. All we could do was to take things as they came and make decisions as required.

We lost no time in eating breakfast and removing ourselves from the sad hotel where we had spent the night. Lunch in Monsieur Senac's fine hotel in Goudet had cost us $6.00. Here in Le Bouchet-Saint-Nicolas, we had received exactly what we paid for. Dinner, overnight, and breakfast for the three of us cost $6.90!

Now we went next door to greet Modestine. The farmer and his family were all standing around telling us what a fine animal she was and how well she had eaten. They refused to take any money for keeping her. Perhaps they all knew by this time she wasn't worth a franc. Quickly, we loaded up and left Bouchet. This time there was no send off because everyone in town was attending a funeral. A very somber omen, we thought.

We had spent the day before entirely on paved roads. To be sure, hardly anyone ever used the roads, but there was always the possibility of someone coming along in case of an emergency. The route had been up and down small mountains until we reached Ville d'Ussel. From there on we had been on a high, dull, bare plateau. This second day we continued on the plateau on unpaved roads. The minute Bouchet was out of sight we were alone in most desolate country. For over two hours we trudged along at an incredibly slow rate. We were able to find out the day before that Modestine's favorite speed was two-and-a-half miles per hour. Although this was pretty darned slow, it was good enough for us if she would keep it up. Well, she either couldn't or wouldn't. On three different occasions during Monday morning, she sat down in the road. Now we talked seriously of giving up. What else could we do?

Towards noon we hit a paved road at the little village of Charbonnières-les-Bains. The people there had read about us in the newspaper, and once more we were greeted and questioned about our journey. Pride is a most amazing emotion. To have listened to us, you would have thought we were having the time of our lives and things just couldn't be better.

While we stood talking to a Mademoiselle Sally, who could speak a little English, a car drove up and stopped.

Printed on the side of the car were the words *La Montagne: Le grand quotidien d'information du Centre*. Camera in hand, out jumped a reporter from this newspaper. He informed us that he had been sent out to find us, interview us, and take our picture. He had been looking for us all morning. That did it. Never for a second did we even suggest that we were considering putting an end to our miseries. In fact, we didn't even suggest we had any miseries. If anyone had bothered to question the reporter about us, it is certain he would have described how jolly we were.[1]

---

[1] However, he got Roberta and Carol's ages wrong.—Ed.

Translated Article from *La Montagne*

A romantic ten-year-old girl, in a charming corner of California, conceived the dream of her life when she read the celebrated story by the Scotsman Stevenson of his picturesque travels through the Cévennes. This story from the previous century swept away the girl who would become Mrs. Gladstone. Today, her dream is a reality for this American woman, accompanied by her daughters Roberta, 19 years old, and Carol, 15 years old.

After traveling in Europe for several months, the three of them arrived last week in Le-Monastier-sur-Gazeille. They explained their project to M. Convers, mayor of the commune, and Doctor Ollier, president of the Syndicat d'Initiative (chamber of commerce). They needed to find a donkey and then they would follow the itinerary of Stevenson from Le-Monastier-sur-Gazeille to Saint-Jean-du-Gard over the rough hills terrain of the Cévennes.

Every year some visitor arrives from overseas, who has contemplated the author's magnificent descriptions, and wishes to make the Stevenson pilgrimage.

Then the job was to find a suitable animal for Mrs. Gladstone. Donkeys are scarce in this region. But they found a female donkey in Chambon-sur-Lignon who was quickly baptized "Modestine," the name of the donkey that accompanied Stevenson.

On Sunday morning, Modestine, fully loaded, in the company of Mrs. Gladstone, Roberta, and Carol, made her departure from Le Monastier. The first day's walk took them to Bouchet-St-Nicolas, where they spent the night. Today they are going toward Pradelles courageously pursuing their goal. We found them as they were leaving Landos.

Mrs. Gladstone, who speaks our language easily, admitted that the first day's walk tired them a little. Up until now Modestine has behaved fairly well, though she is skittish when they have to cross a stream.

The progress of this troupe never fails to excite curiosity, and Mrs. Gladstone, very graciously, struck up conversations with the inhabitants of the villages where she is always warmly welcomed.

Bon Voyage, Mrs. Gladstone, Roberta, and Carol, and choose your best memories to tell Mr. Gladstone and your friends when you return to California.

For the next few hours, we had no opportunity to drop the pose we had set for ourselves. Continuing on the unpaved, dirt road, we passed through a succession of about six tiny villages, repeating our cheerful story over and over again. In Armargiers a pleasant man told us that we could find a cup of coffee at his brother-in-law's café in Landos. In Landos, the brother-in-law was waiting for us, and we had our coffee.

Well, we were making progress along the road. During each of Modestine's collapses, we analyzed her condition carefully. We still had no idea what this behavior was all about. Because with one swift whack and a tug on the lead rope we always got her going again, we felt the situation wasn't desperate. We noticed that before each of her sit-down strikes, she would begin to lower her head. As soon as her nose reached the road, down she would go. We experimented with keeping her head up, and, sure enough, she kept going. We didn't understand this, but, as long as it worked, we were satisfied. After lunch, we experimented again; and, when she started to lower her head, we let her do it. Down she went! Aha! We had asked every farmer we had met for his theory on Modestine's irritating habit.

Several farmers laughed and said, "That's a donkey for you!"

Some of them jokingly suggested we turn her into sausage. We were not amused.

Now we doubted that Modestine had brains enough to play tricks on us. We also hoped she wasn't suffering from the exertion of carrying our packs all day. The truth was we just didn't know what was at the bottom of this annoying and constant delay. Not knowing what would happen next put us under a constant strain, which just added to the fatigue of the long walk.

At Les Uffernets, a small group of farm houses along the road, a pleasant family insisted that we come to their house for coffee. We were relieved to have an excuse to sit down for a while. While our French vocabulary was increasing, we still often found ourselves at a loss for the right word. One word that we had to know was the French word for "hay" as we would have to request this delectable item for Modestine's dinner each night.

I held up some grass and asked in the words that I did know, "What is the word for grass when it is brown and dry?"

Our hostess answered, *"Le fou-enne."*

I wasn't sure how to spell the word, but that's the way it sounded. The magic words *le fou-enne* never failed to obtain the desired menu item for Modestine. Weeks later in Paris when we were telling somebody of the humorous vocabulary we had to use during our trip in the mountains, I mentioned *le fou-enne*. To my amazement and embarrassment, the word for hay turned out to be *les foins;* pronounced as if it were "le fwan" (final *n* silent). We had been given the local mountain pronunciation, which everyone, thank goodness, understood, but it was not pure French.

We were always interested to see the inside of these country farms. They all looked the same on the outside; ancient gray stones, very thick walls, houses, and barns attached in one two-story unit. Their interiors varied with the wealth of the owner, never very great in this part of France. This is the poorest section in all of France, with, we were told, the lowest tax rate. It is solely an agricultural area and this on a very small and poor scale. This family in Les Uffernets had more evidence of wealth than any other we met, but it was still a very minimum amount. Their floors were wooden, but unfinished. The walls were unsurfaced, merely the inside of the gray rocks used to construct the outer walls. A cold water faucet was the only plumbing feature, and the stove burned wood. These houses were built for use but were incidentally very picturesque. As we sat in the kitchen, which also served as the sitting room, we were surrounded by lovely china and copper utensils.

By the time we left the farm, the kitchen was crowded with women and children. As we walked down the road, we heard their good wishes called to us, and suddenly we came to an important decision. No personal hardships would ever lead us to discontinue our journey as planned. The tremendous show of interest, curiosity, and friendship during the past two days added up to encouragement that would keep us going, no matter what happened. We were feeling much better and our sense of humor returned. The next time Modestine started drooping, we let her droop and down she went.

"Modestine, we will give you exactly five minutes!"

Roberta and I lit up cigarettes and watched the clock. In exactly five minutes I administered the stick, Modestine uncoiled herself, and we were off again.

We were now descending slightly from the plateau and the area looked less forbidding. There were a few fields and more and more trees as we continued to go downhill. Late in the afternoon our dirt road reached the paved National Highway leading to Pradelles; we could see the fairly large town of Pradelles halfway down the mountain. With the day's goal in sight finally, we were very cheerful.

"Modestine, you may not lie down in the National Highway!"

We kept her nose up and all went well. We were tired, but eleven miles compared to the previous day's sixteen made a lot of difference.

Pradelles! Windows flew open, people crowded on to the street and followed us. *"Bravo! Les Americaines!"*

What a clamor! We planned to spend the night in the youth hostel, and dozens of people were pleased to lead us there. The warden of the hostel and his wife, Monsieur and Madame Parayre, were called, and we found ourselves in excellent hands. They made all the arrangements for Modestine's bed and board and invited us to their home for an aperitif. We spent a delightful hour with them—adults with aperitifs, children with cookies and milk. They were both teachers as well as house parents for the youth hostel. Madame Parayre had attended teacher's college with Madame Robert of Le Monastier-sur-Gazeille. We would have been pleased to sit there all evening with them except that we had to have dinner and get to bed. Parayre conducted us to a restaurant after having explained where we would sleep. Although the hostel was still closed for the winter, we were being allowed to stay there. That whole evening was a cheerful contrast to the gloom of the previous one at Bouchet. Things were definitely looking up.

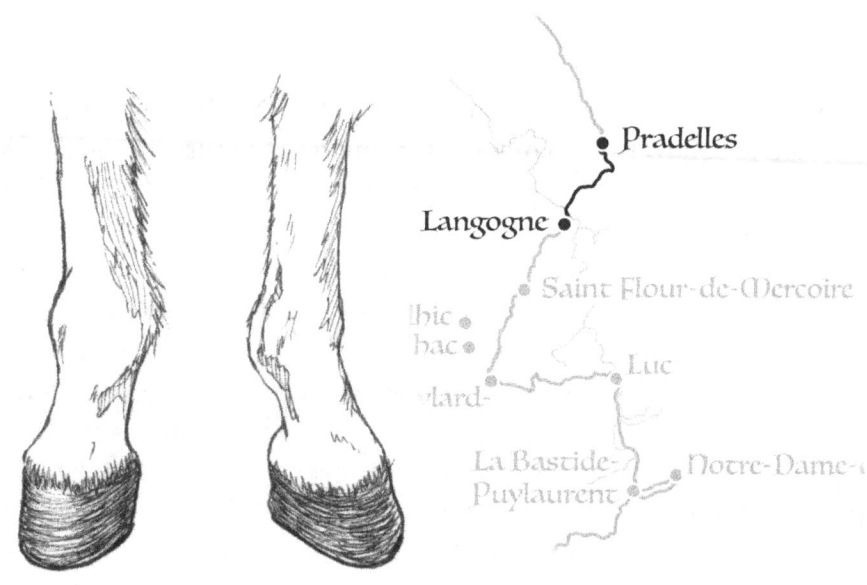

Chapter 6

Dutch Farmer and Donkey Repair

We had sampled youth hostels all over Europe. Our store of memories was stacked full of not only a good night's rest but much hilarity and fun, too. We preferred hostels to hotels whenever we found one, as something or someone invariably turned up to generate a happy event. As a result, we felt very kindly to them.

Waking up that morning (Tuesday, 14 May) we felt a little more rested, a little more comforted than if we had been anywhere else. We took longer than necessary to wash and dress. I think we were all loath to leave one second before we had to. After breakfast in a café, we found the Parayres and prepared to leave. Someone was sent off to bring Modestine to us; everything was so completely arranged for us by the Parayres that we had never seen Modestine's stable in Pradelles. Two little boys were assigned to us to lead us on to the right road to Langogne. We wanted to avoid the National Highway and had decided to follow the old dirt road through the mountain meadows.

Dozens of people stood around watching us as we loaded up Modestine and said our farewells. We were sorry to leave so soon and were most sincere when we said that we hoped to return some other time. Stevenson had used Pradelles as a lunch stop and had gone on to Langogne for the night; we were going to do it the other way round, as it would be the only hostel we could find. Our two young guides set out before us, chattering all the way. They pointed out all the sights of interest. They were proud little boys, proud of their town and proud of their role as guides to *les Americaines*.[1] Shortly, we were on the road, and Langogne was clearly in view down in the valley of the Allier River. Regretfully, our little friends left us, and we were alone.

We felt just fine and not too upset about the two burning questions of the day. The first was the matter of our route after Langogne. We hadn't the foggiest idea where we would spend the night. Stevenson had left Langogne in the morning and proceeded to get lost during the next stage of his trip. After Langogne we would be entering very barren land at relatively high altitudes. Our maps showed very few houses, so not many people lived around there. Stevenson had found this true and also that the few people who lived there were mighty unfriendly and inhospitable, not a very gay prospect for us.

The second burning question was Modestine. Shortly after we left Pradelles, she started to drag her nose on the ground. We gave her her head and, of course, she went down. We had no trouble getting her under way again, but she continued to try to get her nose down. We were fresh and also strong-willed at that early hour, so we took turns holding the guide rope that kept her nose on even keel.

This was slightly annoying, because at least one of us had to concentrate on the rope and nose all the time. There was also the nagging fear that, in spite of this unsatisfactory solution, she might still collapse.

As we came to Langogne, we passed a small farmhouse.

---

1   The boys were in short trousers, a custom that had long since died out in the United States. We asked if they were cold, but they claimed to be warm and seemed a little surprised by the question.—Ed.

From the yard a voice called, *"Bon jour,"* then "Hello!."

"Hello!" we called back in amazement on hearing the greeting in English.

"I didn't think you looked French," he said. "Are you American?"

"Yes, we are; are you French?" we asked. "No, I'm Dutch, but I live here."

Although we were bowled over by this unexpected encounter, we felt that an English-speaking farmer might be able to tell us about Modestine's difficulties.

We lost no time in spilling out the whole tale of woes and then hopefully asked, "Can you tell us what is the matter?"

He didn't answer immediately, but he looked over the silly donkey, asking us various questions. Although he was not a vet, he gave the impression that whatever he said would be exactly right. He seemed very intelligent by the questions he asked and the very deliberate way he thought over the whole matter.

Finally, he reached a conclusion. "It is her feet; she will have to have them fixed."

"Do you mean she will need shoes?"

"No, look how her foot is raised in the front; they will have to be filed even."

"Where can we find someone to do this?" we asked.

"Oh, that is no problem; there are several men in Langogne who can do this."

"Will it take long and cost a lot?"

"Oh, no, it is nothing," he said.

Finding things and getting the simplest things done in a foreign country was always a chore. Finding a foot doctor for a donkey in Langogne did not strike us as a simple matter; but, of course, it had to be done. Relieved and grateful, we took leave of this fine Dutchman, Rombout Hellendorn, and continued down the road.

By this time, we were hungry and because we were certain that nothing could be accomplished during the sacred siesta hours (twelve to two p.m.), we decided to have luncheon. Our moods changed quickly depending on how things were going. Right then, unaccountably, we were in the mood for the best Langogne had to offer. The

Hôtel de la Poste was spangled with the recommendation insignia of all the reliable auto clubs in Europe. That was for us. The clerk at the desk was rather frosty as she showed us where we could tie Modestine in the garage.

Upstairs the dining room was full of white-clothed tables and well-dressed diners who greeted us with curious stares. Our blue jeans seemed out of place for the first time. It didn't matter. The food was excellent (and expensive).

We felt great. Soon enough, however, we descended the stairs to the garage and at the same time came back to reality.

Without knowing the French words for the operation to be performed on our animal or the name of the performer, we were somehow able to indicate what we were looking for. However, we weren't confident about what we would say to this man when we found him.

At a flash the whole state of confusion ended. Looking down the street to which we had been directed, we saw Rombout waiting for us. From that second on we were mere appendages; Rombout took care of everything. One would have thought he had taken a precious child to the doctor instead of some stranger's donkey. After the farrier spent about an hour shaving off Modestine's feet to Rombout's explicit directions, the deed was done. For less than two dollars, we had a new donkey. We were astounded by the change in Modestine's appearance. She stood with her head held high. We thought she even had a new expression on her dumb face. Rombout was our hero.

"Would you like to come to our house to spend the night?" he asked.

Boy, would we ever! It was much too late in the afternoon to think of continuing ten miles off into strange parts. It had been over a week since we had spoken English; the prospect of a few more hours of communication in our own language was welcome, too. Robert Louis Stevenson's problems had led him one way; ours were leading us another. So back to the farm.

Up to that moment, Rombout, though a real friend, had been only a means to solve our problems. Now we began to give some thought to him. We assumed that he had probably married a French girl and that was the reason he was so far from home. He was certainly

Figure 4. Modestine undergoing hoof repair (farrier, Modestine, Betty, and Rombout)

a fine gentleman to have spent so much time on our behalf. By the way he talked, he gave us the feeling that he was pretty well educated, and we wondered why he had chosen to be a farmer.

Rombout had gone ahead on his motorbike; it took us about half an hour to catch up with him at the house. The house had not attracted our attention in the morning, because at first glance it looked exactly like all the other farm houses in the area; gray stone with a red tile roof.

Now, as we approached, we could see that it was smaller than most. On the left half of the building was a door and four gray shuttered windows. On the right side we could see through the open door that the barn (where we would sleep) was attached to the house. We walked into the kitchen, which served not only that purpose but as living room, family room, and work room. A single electric light hung on a wire in the middle of the room. The furnishings consisted of a wood stove, a large table, a few smaller tables, and some chairs. No refrigerator; no sink. Under one table were various size containers of milk.

We entered the house with Rombout, and then we met his wife. Having expected a French farm girl, we were amazed to find Nanette, a young, beautiful Dutch girl. She, too, spoke English and made us feel welcome immediately in our own language.

Perhaps unusual circumstances evoke unusual behavior. In any case, they were so curious to hear about us and what we were doing, and we were so curious to know what a couple of Dutch people were doing in that part of France that at once we embarked on a series of very personal questions to each other. As soon as they heard we were from the San Francisco area, Nanette told us that her brother actually lived in San Francisco with his wife and children! This made us feel almost like members of the family. We sat drinking coffee and talking at a mad rate.

Nanette had come from a professional family in Amsterdam. By the time she married Rombout, he had finished agricultural college, and they decided to go to France and become farmers. Due to a serious overpopulation problem in Holland, the government subsidized citizens who were willing to emigrate. It was for this reason the Hellendorns went to France. We listened to their story and wondered why they would give up the comfort and ease of life in Amsterdam for the rigors of farm life in this God-forsaken mountain region. Suffice here to say they did it and were obviously very content.

During all the time we spent with that family, we observed with amazement and admiration how they managed under the most primitive conditions. We saw Nanette go several hundred yards down the mountainside and return carrying buckets of water. We watched her cook and boil clothing on the temperamental wood stove. Rombout was busy from morning until night milking cows and goats; tending rabbits, chickens, and geese; delivering milk, cheese, and butter on his motorbike; and cleaning and repairing the barn and equipment.

In the midst of all the other work, there were the children to care for. Bernette was three years old; Occo, only six months. I could barely stand to think about the water supply needed just to boil Occo's diapers every day. It was unthinkable that the long trip to the well had to be made through snow in the winter. I guess we were more impressed by the water problem than anything else, except maybe the total lack of a bathroom or even a reasonable facsimile of one.

We spent a happy evening with Nanette and Rombout. When they were occupied with their numerous chores, we looked through their library of books in several languages and listened to classical music from their record collection. We were very grateful to Rombout for knowing what ailed Modestine and what to do about it. We had been asked many times what we would do with Modestine at the end of the trip. Now we knew. We would send her back to the Hellendorns. Her strong back could relieve Nanette and Rombout from many of their backbreaking chores. Also, we could be confident that she would be with friends who would love her and take care of her.

A footnote to this decision came after we had returned home and had telephoned Nanette's brother in San Francisco. He had received a letter from his mother in Holland, which said, "Nanette has written that three Americans traveling with a donkey had visited them and promised to give them the donkey. This is ridiculous; whoever heard of Americans traveling with a donkey! They will never receive that donkey."

Chapter 7

Lost in the Rain

Wednesday morning, 15 May, we awoke about seven in that dark windowless barn. Outside wasn't much lighter, as it was a gray, drizzly day. After dressing we joined the Hellendorns who were already very busy with their endless chores. Rombout had milked the cows and was about to deliver milk to his customers. Nanette was spreading herself very thin, attending to the children, fixing breakfast, starting the laundry to boil on the stove, and starting to make cheese. We helped ourselves to coffee and bread, packed up our belongings, and loaded them onto Modestine's back. None of us had time for prolonged farewells. I think it was in the back of each of our minds that this was not "Goodbye forever," and so our parting was both quicker and easier.

We left the farm at about nine in a cool rain. About one mile down the road, we came to a gas station with restrooms; the lady kindly consented to let us use them even though in Europe this privilege is generally reserved for customers only. Finally, we were able to consider our plans for the day. Robert Louis Stevenson left Langogne with the intention of going to Le Cheylard-l'Évêque. He found the intervening area unmarked, sparsely populated, and above all very desolate. As a result, he became lost and finally spent the night out of doors in the neighborhood of two tiny and unfriendly villages of Fouzilhic and Fouzilhac after being treated dismally by the natives.

Our previous examination of maps had led us to guess that we might meet with similar difficulties trying to find the way through that area. We could see where we wanted to go, but it was not obvious exactly how to get there. We left the road shortly after Langogne and started to follow a path in the general direction of our goal. About an hour later we reached a place called Pont-de-Barret on the map, which consisted of one single house with barn attached.

The family was outside watching our approach with obvious curiosity. As briefly as possible we told them what we were up to and then asked for directions to Fouzilhic and Fouzilhac. They told us it was impossible to go there on the relatively straight line we had selected. They said we had to go back to the main road and then follow some long out-of-the-way route. We asked why we shouldn't go the way we had planned.

They simply shrugged their shoulders and said, *"C'est impossible."*

We thanked them, said goodbye, and, ignoring their advice, proceeded to do what we had planned originally.

Setting our sights in a direct line toward our objectives, we started up a little hill towards some woods. For about ten minutes everything was fine. Then came the trees. They were so close together that Modestine and the packs could not fit between them. We looked at the map and could see that we would add very little distance to the route if we stayed on the edge of the woods and travelled around them. We followed a cow path east of the woods with great difficulty. The path was quite overgrown with a new growth of gorse, and we had to hold the branches apart to permit Modestine to get through. We didn't enjoy this one bit, but at least we were making some progress.

Looking ahead, we could see some open fields and were relieved that this scrubby terrain was coming to an end. It did—at a barbed wire fence. By this time we were very tired and the rain was coming down in sheets. We couldn't go on because we couldn't figure out any way to get Modestine over the fence. We felt we just didn't have the energy to retrace those arduous steps through the brush, but that is what we had to do.

We hoped no one at the farm called Barret saw us returning to our starting point; it was just too embarrassing after what they had told us. Short of returning to the road as we had been directed, there was one more path we could take. We would have to cut a wider swath around the woods and the fenced-in field, but we would still end up going in the right direction. Again, we were on a cow path; this time it was easier footing. Aside from the rain, there was no other problem, and our spirits began to rise again. We had confidence that once we had gotten over the little stream indicated on the map, we could go the rest of the way very quickly. Soon we saw the little river ahead with an old stone bridge across it. Wet, cold, and tired, we looked with despair. The bridge had decayed and broken off in the middle of the river!

It was a very ugly moment. Without repeating who said what, I will say that it was recalled that we had been warned. We were unhappy and uncomfortable and not pleasant to each other for quite some little time. We decided to eat lunch and then follow the farmer's suggestion after all. Nothing except our dispositions improved with full stomachs. Actually, our morale was still pretty low since we faced the embarrassment of admitting our follies over at the Barret farm.

Some vicious fates decided to make even that as unpleasant as possible. As we approached the farm, it started to hail and we were forced to beg for shelter in the barn while suffering abject humiliation at the same time. As soon as the hail reverted to rain, the farmer, taking no chances this time, led us up a path that would take us back to the main road.

After wasting the entire morning wandering aimlessly, we knew we could not reach Fouzilhic and Fouzilhac by night, especially in the wet and cold. So we set out to do what Stevenson had intended to do in the first place: go directly to Cheylard. Less than two miles down the road, we found the dirt road, which after about five miles would take us to Cheylard. We were weary and dejected, but we were slowly able to warm and then kindle a few sparks of humor.

"Mommy, let's stop for a while and do some painting," Carol quipped as the rain poured off her hood into her face.

"Don't be bitter, Carol," Roberta said, "Just think of the charming inn and delicious dinner we're going to enjoy this evening."

Now that was a happy thought and we dwelled on it for some time. I suggested we might find that the hotel was a Logis de France, one of the organization's finest. Rather than stopping to paint, we kept walking and painting in our imagination the picture of the hotel at Cheylard. It would certainly be attractive to look at, probably one of the gray stone buildings with a tiled roof. The family would all come out to greet us and immediately take Modestine off to the barn so that we could go right in to get warmed up. We would find a fire roaring in the large fireplace and hot coffee on the stove. Someone would surely take our wet clothes off to be dried. Our rooms would be attractive and comfortable; there would be a bathroom with flush toilets and showers with quantities of hot water. Next, we each tried to outdo the other on the description of the dinner. A good French dinner with delicious bread and wine is always a matter for eager contemplation.

In the meantime, it had started to hail again, and we were forced for the moment to stop contemplating and consider the present. We had just arrived at the tiny Saint Flour-de-Mercoire. The length of French names is often out of proportion to the named object. Saint Flour consisted of a few houses, a dozen perhaps, and that's all. The familiar red cigar sign hung out in front of one of them. This usually means tabac (tobacco) and occasionally café, too. This appeared to be someone's home, but we knocked on the door anyway. A very pleasant lady came to the door and said she would be happy to give us shelter and a cup of coffee. She also let us put poor Modestine in her barn. What a break we reached there at that moment, because looking out through the window we could see the hailstones, large and ferocious being blown by a strong gale. By the time we had finished our coffee, the hail had reverted to rain once again and the wind had died down a little.

Leaving Saint Flour we saw the sign to Cheylard: six kilometers, or about four miles. That day of aimless wandering around in very disagreeable weather was coming to an end. We recalled the image of the Logis de France hotel we would soon find and trudged on. Even if we had been fresh and rested, if the sun had been shining and the air warm, we would probably not have been much more enthusiastic about those few miles. We had climbed a thousand or more feet from the valley of the Allier River and were now on a sharp, narrow ridge. The vegetation was sparse and the terrain very rocky. We could look down on each side of the ridge and see gray mist churning about on the windy mountain slopes. The narrow dirt road on top of the ridge was completely at the mercy of the wind, and we felt we could easily be blown off. By this time, it was late afternoon and it had become very cold. The rain, which we had seen turn to hail twice already, now turned to snow.

Poor little donkey! The snow and wind were too much for her and she walked slower and slower. The snow piled up on her back and also on her closed eyes. We were soaked and freezing. Carol didn't have gloves, but Roberta's and mine were so wet and cold that they were worse than nothing. We pulled our hoods as tightly together as possible, so that only our eyes and noses were exposed. For once, all of us were silent.

After nearly two hours of this, we finally saw Cheylard way down the mountain in front of us. Once again, the image of the Logis de France hotel came to mind. Roberta bravely volunteered to walk on ahead and make all arrangements at the hotel. Because of Modestine we were never able to exceed the two-and-a-half miles per hour speed. Carol and I followed along at this rate and at last arrived in Cheylard.

The first thing to greet us was Roberta standing in the middle of the street. I left Carol with Modestine and ran over to her.

"Where is the hotel? Have you met the mayor? Is everything arranged?"

Roberta was almost in tears. "Oh, Mommy, the mayor lives miles out of town; there is no hotel, no restaurant, nothing!"

Carol joined us and heard the news. "We're soaking wet, freezing, starving, and exhausted. What are we going to do?"

I certainly didn't have an answer to her question. I just knew we had to do something. Also, we had to do it here; there was no other place to go.

A red cigar hung out in front of one of the houses, and I went over and knocked. The door was opened. We tied Modestine to a tree and went inside. A small group of unsmiling and incurious people were in the room. This was the first time that no one seemed to wonder who we were and what we were doing.

I went over to Madame and in my most charming, friendly, and smiling way asked, "Is there a hotel here?"

"*Non*," she answered.

"Would you have room for us?"

"*Non*."

"Is there someone who would let us stay in his barn?"

At this point Monsieur stepped forward and said, "*Moi*."

Now we were getting somewhere. There was really some urgency for us to get settled in some way and get out of our wet clothes, so I tried to get things moving. Finally, we were conducted about a block away to a large, solidly built barn. En route I asked if Modestine could find food and shelter there, too, so first we took her to a stall well supplied with hay and water. Then we went out of doors and around to the upstairs hayloft, which was happily both dry and warm. We deposited our packs on the floor and went back to the café with Monsieur.

Although we had solved the problem of where to spend the night, we still weren't in good shape. There was the little matter of food, but of immediate concern was that we were still wet and cold. As soon as we reentered the café, we removed our jackets and shoes and socks. There were two meager sources of heat in the room. One was a tiny wood stove, and the other, the wood fire in the cook stove. We drew chairs to the small stove and tried to thaw out. No one was paying much attention to us. The room appeared to be a combination public café and private kitchen.

Various people wandered in, had a glass of wine, and then left. The family consisted of Mother, Father, and daughter Josette, eighteen years old. In addition, there was an old man with a dog who seemed to be their shepherd.

The room itself was very plain. On one side were two bare wooden tables with chairs; this was the café. On the other side was a sink, the two stoves, and another table for the family. It is the usual thing over much of Europe for a small town to have only one telephone. Cheylard's telephone was in a closet off this room. Occasionally, the phone would ring and someone would go off to fetch the person for whom the call was.

All conversation was at a minimum, and there was a spiritless, joyless atmosphere in the room. We ourselves were certainly quiet for some time. We had a bit of recovering to do before we could even try to talk and smile again. Having observed the general lack of sympathy for our plight, we wondered how we were ever going to get any further help, such as supper. It occurred to me we might impress these people with one of the newspaper articles that had appeared about us. I didn't relish the cold, dark walk to the barn, but I decided to go and get the newspaper. When I returned, I showed it to Madame. She and her daughter had been talking to a couple of women who had come in. Now we saw the first sign of animation. She read the story and excitedly showed it to her daughter and friends. Then she gave it to her husband. Then she came over to us and started to talk. She took our wet socks and jackets, hung them on hangers over the stove, and arranged our shoes near the two wood fires. Although supper was utmost in my mind, I didn't want to press her just yet. As this was a café, it was a legitimate request to ask her for coffee, and she was happy to get it for us.

During the next hour we drank coffee, warmed ourselves at the stove, and waited. Madame was busy in the kitchen end of the room with preparations for the family supper. I kept hoping she would ask if we cared to eat something. She never did. There was something about the whole sequence of events since we had arrived that made me loath to ask her. Mainly, I feared she would say *"Non"* again, and then what would we do?

When I realized I really had no alternative, I got up my courage and asked, "Do you have enough soup for us, too?"

"Oui," she said, and that was the end of our suspense.

It was a thick potato soup, not too tasty, but filling and hot. Later, she put some sausage and bread on the table, so in the end we had enough to eat. Just as soon as we were finished, we told them we were so tired that we would go to bed immediately. Monsieur got a flashlight and said he would come with us. But—there was one more important thing.

"*Avez-vous une toilette, Madame?*" ("Do you have a toilet, Madam?")

"*Non.*" ("No.")

"*Un cabinet?*" (A cabinet?")

"*Non.*" ("No.")

"*Un 'W. C.'?*" ("A 'W. C.' (or water closet"?)

"*Non.*" ("No.")

We were getting experienced with this sort of thing and knew we could find a corner of the barn that would suit our purposes.

The barn was excellent for everything we needed. It was well stocked with hay, and, before Monsieur left us, he kindly forked a huge pile of it down off the stack. It was considerably warmer in the barn than in the café, because the heat from the bodies of the cows, goats, sheep, and our Modestine was a much more efficient furnace than the two feeble wood stoves. The animals, each making its own noise, were downstairs. There was a light in our room, so we could see what we were doing. We made a thick mattress out of hay, put down our sleeping bags, and then piled liberal amounts of hay on top for additional warmth. We each staked out a corner of the barn for our private uses. It was certainly no Logis de France, but in the end we had everything we needed.

On Thursday, 16 May, we woke up one at a time; our eyes attracted to the window in the barn wall.

"It's still raining."

"I can't move."

"I'm going back to sleep."

I lay listening to these whispered comments of the children before they knew I was awake. It was certainly warm and comfortable, and the thought of going out into another wet, cold day was more than I could stand.

Especially after the hardships of the previous four days, how could I ask these girls to plod on in that weather?

I joined in the conversation. "What do you think about staying here today?"

"Good night, I'm going to sleep right now," said Roberta.

"What will we eat?" Carol wanted to know.

"Well, we have plenty of cheese, butter, and chocolate," I said, "also some leftover bread and three oranges. Maybe Madame can give us something, too, if she knows we're staying."

And so it was decided.

For a few hours we dozed, nibbled at food, and wallowed in the warm, soft hay. The day before, our vision of a Logis de France hotel was our conception of luxury.

But today resting in a warm, dry barn, seemed the very height of luxury itself. We laughed and we sang and we played Twenty Questions. We thought of all the people back home who would never believe it, even if they could see us right now. We compared Cheylard in each detail to the United States, especially contrasting certain plumbing arrangements with the complete lack of them. In the midst of total hilarity, we looked up and saw that Madame and her daughter had come in and were standing looking at us. It was obvious that they didn't know what to think about us, but, never having had three American ladies in their barn before, how could they? Madame asked if she could bring us anything; and, although a cup of coffee would have been the most welcomed gift in the world, we could not bring ourselves to say so. Instead, we asked if there was anyone in town who baked bread. There was, and brave, brave Carol volunteered to go out and buy a loaf.

Having plenty to eat for luncheon, we had no reason to leave our nest all afternoon and we didn't. We hoped that Madame would provide dinner of some sort, if possible without our having to ask her. Late in the afternoon we dressed and went over to the café. We had coffee and we sat and watched the comings and goings of various people. A sudden gathering of people in the street caught our eyes through the window. A small truck had arrived, and it turned out to be an itinerant grocery store. Again, no one was curious or even friendly; they just ignored us. We bought some oranges and a basket of pansy plants that we presented to Madame. She seemed very pleased.

As the dinner hour approached, and we had not been asked to share in it, I was forced once again to ask: "Is there enough for us too?"

This time the answer was, "Maybe."

I sat down at a table with the girls, and we waited, not being sure what would happen next. Fortunately, the same procedure as the night before was followed; the only difference was the thickness of the soup: it was very watery.[1]

---

[1] One of the surprises I find in looking back on this trip over fifty years later is that, despite the concerns my mother expressed in this chapter, my sister and I were completely engaged with the trip. We thought of it as "our" trip, not "her" trip; and, despite our grumbles about being cold or hungry, we enjoyed the adventures and didn't wish to be anywhere else.—Ed.

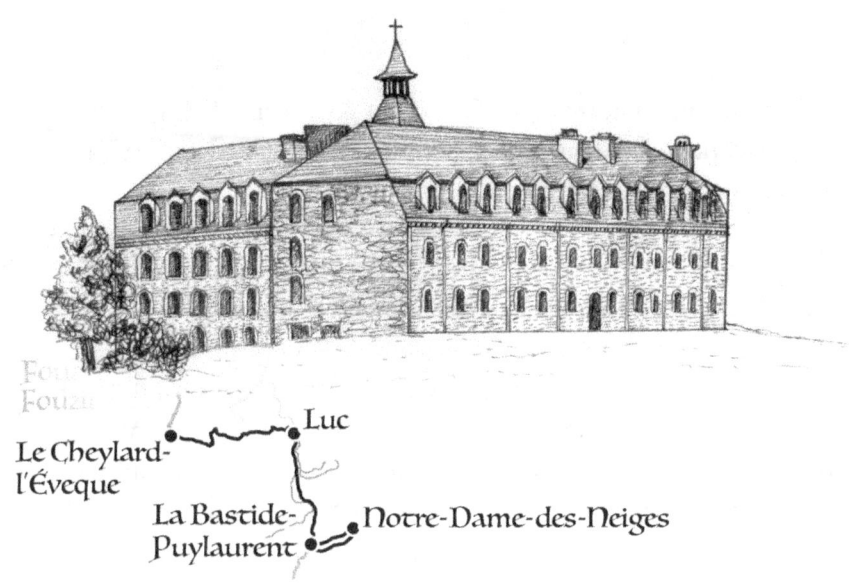

Chapter 8

Monastery

Silently we followed Josette, our host's daughter, out of the village. It was a silent kind of day (Friday, 17 May). The sky was gray and a misty rain was falling. Our path led us by a tiny river through an open meadow at the edge of the forest. Soon we could see a collection of gray stone houses at the top of a small mountain; this was Les Pradels. Josette[1] felt confident we could find our way up there, and so she left us.

For the first time since Le Cheylard-l'Évêque, we started to talk. Talking started our thinking, and we talked and thought about Cheylard for the next couple of hours.

Stevenson had said of Cheylard, "Candidly, it seemed little worthy of all this searching."

He added, "Why anyone should desire to visit either Luc or Cheylard is more than my much-inventing spirit can suppose."

---

1 After Betty returned to the Cévennes in 1965, she took Josette for a vacation on the Côte d'Azur.—Ed.

Yet for our own reasons, Cheylard represents the strangest part of our adventures. I think this is because Cheylard took us farthest away from our accustomed life.[2]

When we reached Les Pradels, we found the narrow dirt road that our map indicated would take us to Le Luc-en-Provence. We noted the wayside chapel, also on our map. One man driving a most ancient vehicle was on his way into the village; he was the last sign of human life we saw during the next two hours. Although the Earth is round and there is no real end to it, I suggest we can call this part of the Cévennes "The End of the World." Rocks and scrubby underbrush stretch in all directions. There is not even the ruin of a house to indicate that man ever tried to exist there.

By noon we had reached the edge of this dull plateau and were able to look way down the mountain at Luc. We were already starting to feel hungry and the sight of our lunch stop increased our hunger. At this point the map showed that the road would follow a zigzag route. It was usually comforting to find any accurate comparison between the map and our actual location, but not this time. Luc is a long, narrow town lining the banks of the Allier River. Our first sight of it had been its extreme northern point, which was dominated by the ruins of an ancient chateau crowned with an eighty-five-year-old statue of Our Lady. The statue had been consecrated the very week Stevenson had been there.

As we followed our first zig toward the south, we were interested to see what the rest of Luc looked like. On our first northward turn on the zag, we were amused to see Our Lady come back into view. By the time we were about to commence the second full zig and zag, we tried to find a more direct route by which to descend. We were starving, and we could see it would take at least an hour to execute the whole series of turns on the road. If it had not been for Modestine, we could have

---

2 In *Travels with a Donkey,* the previous quotations are followed by some of Stevenson's most celebrated lines: "I travel not to go anywhere, but to go. I travel for travel's sake. The great affair is to move; to feel the needs and hitches of our life more nearly; to come down off this feather-bed of civilization and find the globe granite underfoot and strewn with cutting flints."—Ed.

tumbled down the steep, rocky incline, if necessary by the seat of our pants, but our dainty lady could never have made it. This was one of the moments when we did not love Modestine. We felt the least she could do was to increase her pace to compensate for our suffering, but she did not see it that way. Modestine caused us further delay in eating lunch when we finally did arrive at Luc.

We were in the process of tying her to a tree in a little grassy spot, when a man came storming out of a house across the street saying, "You can't put that donkey there!"

We apologized and asked him very sweetly if he could suggest a place to leave her. After much conversation and our almost collapsing with hunger, the man became very amiable and said we could leave her there after all. He even brought her hay from his barn. And so we went to a café and had luncheon.

We aroused all the usual curiosity of the others in the little café. One of the men had read Stevenson's book, and the others had heard about it. Soon we were all laughing and chatting about our adventures. After lunch Carol went over to check on Modestine while Roberta and I paid our respects to the mayor. She was delighted to see us. She spent five minutes trying to tell us about the United States. It turned out Cooper had just completed his twenty-two turns round the earth, and she thought it was a great thing.[3] It took a while until she figured out some simple vocabulary that we would understand. Before we left her, she pointed out the empty lot where once had stood the inn where Stevenson had spent the night.

Now we were once again walking along the Allier River. Stevenson's curiosity about Cheylard had led him and then us on a miserable detour from Langogne to Luc. It would have been a short, pleasant walk along the river between those two towns, but we would have missed the opportunity of having so much to complain about.

By this time, we found ourselves under blue sky and bright sunshine. The river valley was covered with green grass and green trees.

---

3   Gordon Cooper was the astronaut in command of Mercury MA-9, the last of the Mercury missions flown by NASA as part of its effort to put a man on the moon.—Ed.

As we were walking along a main road, we encountered numerous people. An elderly couple leading an ox cart stopped. They were killing themselves with laughter when they saw us.

The man called, "Do you want to swap your donkey for our oxen?"

Cars slowed down to watch us; everyone laughed and waved. One car stopped altogether and a man came over to us.

"Are you following Stevenson's route?" he asked.

He told us he owned a hotel in La Bastide-Puylaurent and would be honored if we would spend the night there as his guest. We reminded him that Stevenson had spent the night at the Trappist monastery, L'Abbaye Notre Dame des Neiges (Abbey of Our Lady of the Snows), and we hoped to do likewise.

"Do you think the monks will permit us to stay there?"

"Oh, yes; they maintain a *hostellerie* (hostelry or inn) for travelers. You must stop at my hotel first, and I will telephone to Notre Dame and ask them."

This is just what we did, and Monsieur Galière was assured that we would be able to stay at the monastery. After having a cup of coffee with him, we set out for Notre Dame.

In December when we had gone to Le Monastier-sur-Gazeille, we had driven by La Bastide. We had been most anxious not to see any more of the Cévennes than we had to at the time because we wanted everything to be a surprise later on. Notre Dame was the only exception. We had taken the short detour through the pine forest, along the snowy road, just to take a peek. This part of the trip had touched our curiosity more than anything else. Up to now monks and monasteries had been part of our lives only once before. All we knew about these monks was that they were Trappists who had taken a vow of silence. They hadn't been very silent when Stevenson had visited them, but we had no idea how our presence would affect them.

A few miles past La Bastide, we came to the white statue of Our Lady of the Snows, which marked the beginning of the road down to the religious community. Nothing in the world could have changed our minds about our present destination, but we slowed down to postpone our arrival as long as possible. We suddenly realized that we hadn't the foggiest idea about what we might be getting ourselves into. For instance, what do you do when confronted with a monk who might not be allowed to speak to you? We were certain that the community had spokesmen who could deal in plain talk with the outside world, but how should we behave? The more we wondered, the more we worried; and soon we were wishing we had planned to stay at Monsieur Galière's more worldly Hôtel des Pins in La Bastide.

At last we reached the end of the road, and the various buildings of which the community was composed lay before us. To the right were some buildings that looked like houses. On the left were barns and sheds. Beyond and at a higher level were the chapels and their adjoining structures. We walked into the barnyard and immediately a workman came over to us. He was not a monk, he could talk, and what is more he seemed to expect us. Several other men came over and at once unloaded Modestine and led her to the cleanest stall so far. They gave her hay and water without our suggesting it, and then they asked us if we would like a glass of milk.

The adjoining barn was filled with the most beautiful cows I have ever seen. Each had her name printed above her stall. The barn was spotlessly clean, and it was equipped with electric milking machines. The monks were obviously in the dairy business and they certainly knew their business better than anyone else we had seen in the Cévennes so far. We were still a little too awed to think of asking questions about this enterprise, but we wondered whether they believed in pasteurizing milk. The milk we drank was warm; right from the cow. As soon as we were given our drink, our friend excused himself and told us to wait there.

About five minutes later he returned, accompanied by one of the monks. Before we had time to get ourselves worried all over again, we were exuberantly welcomed by a very smiling Père Émile, not at all silent. He was delighted to meet us. He congratulated us for our fortitude taking such a trip. But he had very bad news for us. It was out of the question for us to spend the night at the hostellerie. He broke the news to us so diplomatically that we understood perfectly without having our feelings hurt. He was at a loss to understand how anyone could have said that we could stay there. While the hostellerie was open to all men who sought its comfort, it was totally unacceptable to have women there. Fortunately, though, Modestine was immune from this prohibition, so she was permitted to stay. Père Émile phoned Monsieur Galière and asked him to drive over to get us. While we were waiting, we had a most jolly conversation.

We told Père Émile about a young college professor from Brazil we had encountered in the ruins of Mycenae in Greece. Without knowing one more thing about him, we had invited him to spend the week with us since our plans were similar. For seven exciting and happy days, we wandered through the remains of ancient Greek civilization. Argos, Tiryns, Olympia, and Delphi were our destinations. Our friend, Eric Acquino, had never heard of the youth hostel organization, but he was a good sport and willing to share the hostel's minimum accommodations with us. Sadly, we parted at the end of the week, as we had become very good friends. Unexpectedly, his plans and ours changed, and two weeks later we encountered him in Rome by chance. It was in a museum. Roberta thought it was Eric but doubted what she saw because this man was dressed as a priest. But it was Eric and it also was a priest. He had not wished to put a damper on us by revealing that he was a Franciscan Father. Père Émile was delighted with this story; I think he wished he had been Eric. He asked Roberta if Eric had asked her to marry him.

"No, of course not."

By this time the car came from the hotel and we departed. The contrast between the barn at Cheylard and the Hôtel des Pins in La Bastide struck us as immensely funny. Potato soup one night and vichyssoise the next. No plumbing facilities in Cheylard, and, wonder of wonders, hot showers in La Bastide. It was nicely timed for us—about the middle of our trip, because this was the only bath we encountered in the Cévennes.

After dinner that evening, we had coffee with Monsieur Galière. He showed us the scrapbook on others who had taken Stevenson's trip, including Mr. White and Vera Singer. Madame Robert had told us about them when we were in Le Monastier. They had each done the trip alone with a donkey. Monsieur Galière had quite a bit of contempt for Miss Singer since her trip was a huge publicity stunt. Her lodging was arranged for her ahead of time and everyone had been informed of her complete plans. There was a huge reception for her when she finally reached Saint Jean-du-Gard. We had encountered many people so far who had remembered her. As near as we could tell, they were the only ones who had ever taken the whole trip exactly the way Stevenson had. We heard that some Americans had done it on horseback, no donkey; that someone had tried it on a motorcycle. Evidently, many people drove to many of the points in cars, but even a Jeep would have difficulty following the exact route through the mountains. Certainly nothing with wheels could have maneuvered itself from Cheylard to Les Pradels, although a Jeep could certainly take the road from there to Luc.

Monsieur Galière was so happy to have us that we felt we were doing him a favor by staying there. True to his word, he did not charge us for the room and the showers, but we did have to pay for our meals. What a bargain! The meals alone came to much more than room and board cost us during the entire journey, but there was no question about its being worth it. It was not usually our luck to be so warm, comfortable, and well fed. Our only regret had been not staying at Notre Dame.

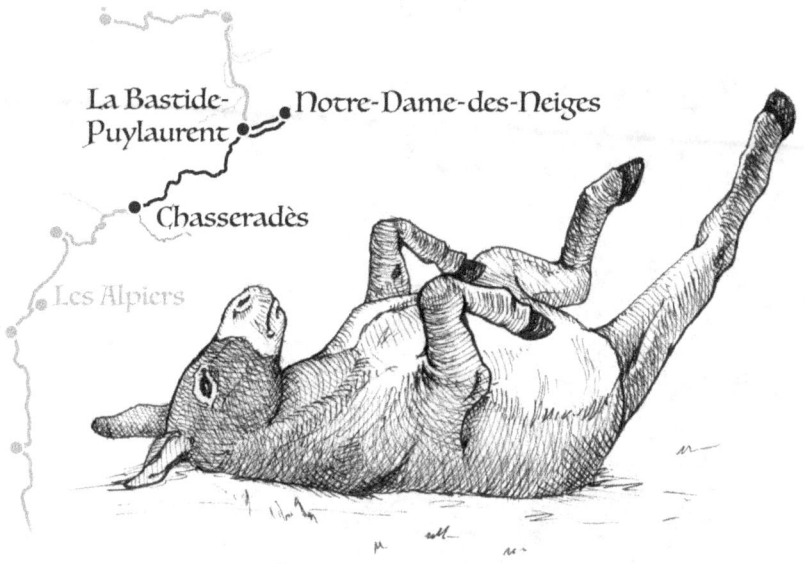

Chapter 9

Dubious Directions

We stayed at the Hôtel des Pins in La Bastide-Puylaurent until after lunch on Saturday, 18 May, and then walked back to the monastery. We felt so carefree walking along at our gait, not Modestine's, for a change. Although we never had to pick up Modestine and carry her, she was some kind of burden, and I don't just mean a beast of burden. Some nights it was sheer torture to have to stand on our aching feet a while longer until we had discovered some suitable lodging for Modestine. She slowed us up. She kept us on curving paths when the straightaway would have shortened our route. We had to worry about her meals; we could never stop for lunch until we had found a satisfactory grazing spot for her. We picked smooth paths for her delicate little feet. We were forever fussing over her, and at the same time we griped about all the trouble she caused us. Since we derived so much pleasure out of the negative aspects of traveling with a donkey, we chose to overlook the advantages. The poor little thing did more than a day's work toting our gear. We did have to

Figure 5. Carol, Betty, Modestine, and Roberta at Hôtel des Pins

admit, too, that her very presence in our entourage was the single most entrancing attraction to everyone who laid eyes on us. Aside

Figure 6. At Notre Dames de Neiges, unnamed workman, Père Emile, Roberta, Betty, Modestine, and Carol

from enjoying having a big fuss made over us, people were more inclined to help us because of the donkey, and there were times when we had to depend on that.

We pretended she was glad to see us when we took her from the stall at the monastery and tied her up in a patch of tulips. For all we knew she hoped she'd never see us again. We spied Père Émile on the side lawn of the hostellerie flying along behind an electric lawnmower. He looked like a huge bird with his robes flapping in the breeze. Laughing as usual, he came over to us and suggested that we go around to the monastery shop. Perhaps we would like some souvenirs and the Father who tended the shop could speak some English.

We waited our turn while a family purchased some religious items and had them blessed by the monk. We bought some postcards and an illustrated booklet about Notre Dame. After a brief conversation with the monk, we went back to the hostellerie. Monsieur Galière had driven over and wanted to take pictures of us.

After the photographic session, we were invited to have an aperitif before our departure. These Trappists were very industrious. In addition to their modern dairy operations, they raised grapes and made wine. For Carol's benefit, Père Émile served us a very mild and sweet muscatel. It was very good, but teetotaling Carol didn't like it.

After several toasts and lengthy farewells, we were ready to leave Notre Dame. Roberta untied Modestine and, for the only time during the two and a half weeks we spent with that young lady, she took off like a shot. We ran and laughed so hard that we could hardly regain our breath. Our acquaintance with Père Émile and the others at Notre Dame had dispelled all our qualms about the mysteries of monks and Trappists in particular. Modestine, on the other hand, evidently had some reason to wish to escape in a big hurry.

We walked a few blocks down to the Allier and then took the level road along the banks of the river. Only six miles to go! But at the end of the first mile, we were already tired. Then we realized what had happened. After a whole day of doing nothing, we were so relaxed that our muscles couldn't hold us up. Also, the easy prospect of six miles compared to the longer distances we had become accustomed to was only an illusion. We felt we could never make it. A weary two-and-a-half hours later, we arrived at the Hôtel de la Gare in Chasseradès, which Monsieur Galière had recommended.

The Hôtel de la Gare was a simple, but very comfortable, hotel. We had two rooms and were delighted to find up-to-date and thoroughly acceptable plumbing arrangements.

Our innkeeper was Madame Saint-Jean, who did everything she could to make us feel at home. She was willing to have Modestine in her garage but thought it would be warmer for her in the little shack at the railroad station. We went over to investigate. The stationmaster, who was the only one around, seemed to think that his shack was the best stable in the world for Modestine. He took us over to the tiny, dark, dirty little building and tried to convince us that he could fix it up just wonderfully for our friend. All we cared about was getting Modestine indoors out of the cold and providing her with sufficient food. He pointed out all the delectable long grass we could pluck and put into the hut, and then he stood there and watched us for fifteen minutes while the three of us stacked grass on the floor of the shack. We glared at him from time to time, but he didn't seem inclined to help us or feel ashamed over not helping us.

While we had been hard at work preparing Modestine's lodgings, she was peacefully grazing tied up to Madame Saint-Jean's front fence. We decided to put off as long as possible locking her up for the night, so we left her there while we went in for dinner. A little while later, we happened to look out, and what a sight we saw! Modestine was on her back; all four legs sticking straight up and she was rolling from side to side in the dirt. We had never seen her look so happy before, and we roared with laughter at the comical picture.

After a simple but perfectly prepared meal, we sat in the dining room talking to Madame Saint-Jean. The stationmaster was the only other person there. They were very curious about us and were pleased to hear about our trip. In our turn, we had some questions.

Since we had left Le Cheylard-l'Évêque, everything had gone very smoothly for us. Modestine was completely free of her earlier troubles. For three days we hadn't had to consult the map, much less worry about getting lost. In spite of the unexpectedly difficult walk from La Bastide to Chasseradès, the whole day had been delightful. We were still enjoying it. Now, however, we needed to come down to earth and face the next phase of the journey.

Although Stevenson's entire route was in the mountains, three particular mountains were higher than the rest. The two most rugged of these lay directly ahead of us. In fact, we could see the whole of the Montagne du Goulet from the hotel in Chasseradès; it looked tremendous. We were going to climb all the way up and down it the next day. On the following day, Montagne de la Lozère, the highest mountain in the Cévennes, would be our goal. We had always known that these two days in a row would challenge the fullest extent of our strength. Our ability to endure the rigors of past days left us questioning our

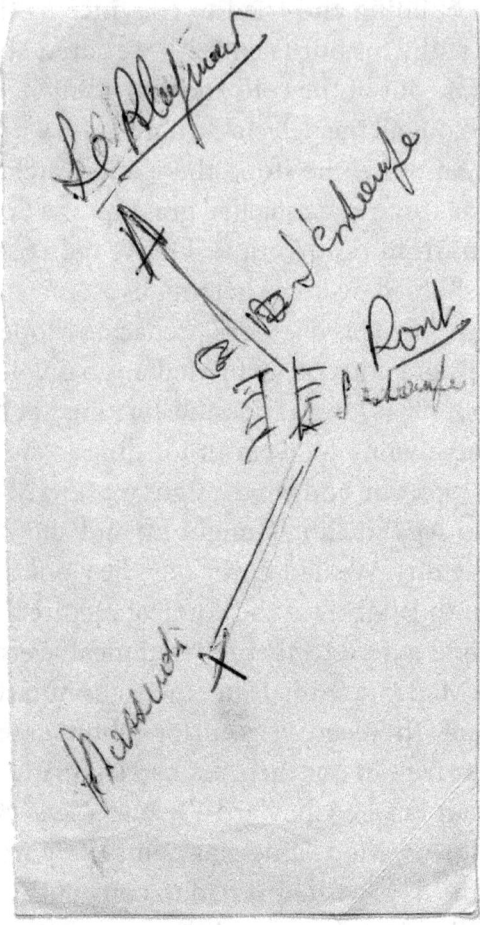

Figure 7. Map of confusion

chances of conquering the really tough mountains. Our doubts were strengthened even farther by the knowledge that we would not always be on marked roads. If we had to add getting lost again to the arduous task of a long ascent and descent, we were in for trouble.

It occurred to us that the stationmaster might be familiar with the Goulet.

"Can you suggest a road for us to follow tomorrow on the mountain?" I asked, pushing our map towards him.

"Oh, yes," was the booming, confident reply. "You take the road to Mirandol, you see?"

Yes, I could see; it was plainly marked on the map.

"Now you cross the river on the bridge, see?"

Again I could see.

"Now you find this little path that goes up the mountain," then turning again to Madame Saint-Jean, he requested a paper and pencil. Being thus supplied, he started over again. "Stay on the road until Mirandol." He drew a line.

"Cross the river; there is a bridge." He drew a line at right angles to the first one.

"Now you find this little path." A long wisp of a line was added to the others. "There, you see?"

I could see that I knew exactly what we knew before by examining the map. I tried one last time.

"What do we do when we reach the end of the path? It just seems to come to an end," I said, pointing to the middle of a completely unmarked area.

"I don't know," he admitted sadly.

I felt I had wounded his ego, so I thanked him as sincerely as I could and invited him to have some wine with us.

The girls and I continued the conversation in English.

"He was a big help!" Carol said.

"What worries me is not the question of finding our way, but why does that path end?" Roberta wondered.

"That's a good question; maybe you can go so far and no farther."

The map was colored solid green at that point, which meant woods.

"Remember going to Cheylard, we couldn't get Modestine between the trees?" Carol recalled.

I said, "We could bring an axe and chop down some trees."

They groaned.

"Well, let's go to bed and worry about it tomorrow," I suggested.

We folded our map, ceremoniously put the stationmaster's diagram on top, thanked him again for his "help," and retired.

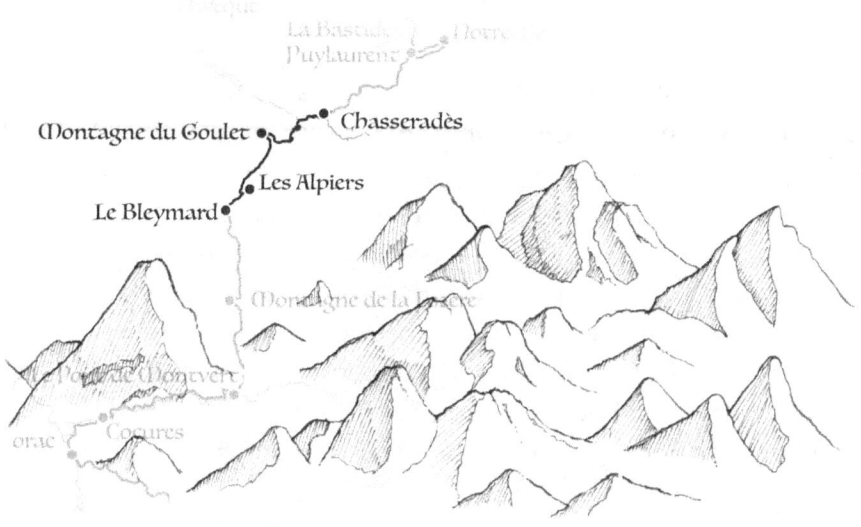

Chapter 10

Facing the Mountains

Our state of mind upon awakening each morning was better or worse depending on what faced us that day. That Sunday morning, 19 May, in Chasseradès, we were subdued with the quietness of the countryside and imbued with the awe of the two great mountains that now lay in our path. We were rested, and our aches and sores were at a minimum; but we had doubts about our ability to climb up and down two such enormous mountains two days in a row. We could see the Montagne du Goulet across the valley; it looked mighty tough to us. We couldn't see Montagne de la Lozère yet, but we knew it was the highest mountain in the Cévennes. We not only doubted whether we would be able to get ourselves up and over each of these mountains, but we also had fears about finding the way.

Stevenson's account of his two days in these parts gave us a number of clues. He said there were places without marked paths. Our map confirmed this unhappy fact. We had had one taste of losing our way, and the prospect of another was grim. No one minds a few extra miles one way or the other in a car; but, when feet start to hurt and you are very weary, each unnecessary hundred yards is a calamity. Our goal that night was Le Bleymard; there were no other refuges for travelers in between. All our doubts and fears notwithstanding, we never for a minute considered not going on. In fact, as the hour of departure arrived, we were in a state of excitement and curiosity about what was going to happen next.

Madame Saint-Jean was very concerned about our food supply because there would be no place to obtain any provisions all day. She went over it carefully, adding a few things from the hotel. She had been a charming hostess.

We retrieved Modestine, none the worse for wear, from her nasty little shack at the station. By nine o'clock on that warm, sunny day, we slowly started down the road. For a couple of miles we stayed on the National Highway. We left it at Mirandol. Mirandol was a cluster of tightly shuttered, gray stone houses and barns. It looked deserted, but we suspected that we were not passing unobserved. In fact, one entire family came out and someone called *"Comme Stevenson!"* ("Like Stevenson!"), and we had a pleasant chat with them about possible routes over the mountain. *Comme Stevenson,* we crossed the Le Chassezac River at this point and found the narrow dirt road that the Mirandol family had suggested we follow.

For a short time, we followed the river, which was hundreds of feet down in a narrow gorge. We felt gay enough to be corny as we exclaimed over the "gorgeous gorge" and went on in a happy and light frame of mind. We passed another collection of buildings that was marked *L'Estampe* (the stamp); very good, so had Stevenson.

Our first hour had been very easy; well-marked roads through grassy meadows. Now we began what Stevenson had referred to as "a steep ascent." Modestine's accustomed pace, which never varied, was perfect for this part of the trip. We enjoyed wandering along through the wooded slopes. We became more and more exhilarated with the increasing scope of the dramatic view behind us. The higher we climbed, the more the panorama of the northern Cévennes stretched out. In the beginning, we could see only the tiny valley of the Le Chassezac and the area around Chasseradès. Next, we could see over the top of the smaller mountains on the edge of the valley. By the time we reached the summit, we could see valleys and their surrounding mountains for as far as the eye could see. Although in very slow motion, this gradually enlarging of the length and breadth of the mountain ranges was like a motion picture.

Towards noon we started to feel hungry. There was no reason not to stop at any given point, because there were many grassy places for Modestine's lunch under the trees, that being our only prerequisite for a dining room. We did not stop yet, however. Once we had reached the Montagne du Goulet and started winding up the narrow road, we could no longer see its peak. The warm air, the blue and sunny sky, and the continual excitement of the magnificent views had completely shut out any pessimism about that day. A mountain is a compelling challenge. Once you decide to climb it, nothing will deter you from reaching the top. Anyway, that's the way we felt. We expected to find ourselves at the peak each time we went around a bend in the road. Hungry as we were, we could not stop climbing until we reached the summit.

It isn't always possible to know the precise spot that can accurately be called the summit. Some round, rolling mountains have no precise summit. The cone-shaped volcanic mountains leave no question about this point. As we had seen from Chasseradès, the Montagne du Goulet did have a definite peak. We had not a single doubt when we finally found ourselves standing on top of it. The same tremendous expanse of mountain ranges that had thrilled us all morning now stretched out to all the other points of the compass. The magnitude of this great expanse took our breath away. It was the prize for the effort of three hours of climbing. But the prize, alas, was spoiled, and we groaned instead of cheering. Many, many miles away, but directly in front of us, we saw Montagne de la Lozère for the first time. It was tremendous as we knew it would be, but, horror of horrors, it was covered with snow. How were we ever going to propel Modestine, not to mention ourselves, over that obstacle?

The problem formed the substance of our lunchtime conversation. Although we felt it would be like cheating, it was possible to go around the mountain. There were clearly marked good roads on the map that could lead us in a circle around to Le Pont-de-Montvert on the other side of Montagne de la Lozère. This was a most unappealing idea, as it would take us three days instead of one, but especially as it would sidestep us completely from Stevenson's route. As it was nonsense to consider ourselves beaten before we had even tried to get over Montagne de la Lozère, we decided to worry about it tomorrow. Today was too pleasant to spoil.

It had certainly not been too difficult climbing the Goulet. The weather and scenery were more than anyone could ask for. Looking out over the seemingly never-ending chains of mountains, we sang "The Bear Went over the Mountain."

> The bear went over the mountain,
> The bear went over the mountain,
> The bear went over the mountain
>   To see what he could see.
>
> And all that he could see,
> Was the other side of the mountain,
> The other side of the mountain,
> The other side of the mountain,
>   Was all that he could see.

We had never realized how true that song could be if you were a mountain-climbing bear. Anyway, we had climbed one mountain to see what we could see and we hoped to climb the other tomorrow. We were in a light hearted and hopeful state of mind as we started down the Goulet. True to Stevenson and the map, there was no clear-cut route down.

At the summit were a jumble of trails leading in all directions, but none of them continuing for very long. Le Bleymard was almost directly southwest of us, but we couldn't see it. We did see the National Highway, which even in Stevenson's day went from Villefort to Mende. Although the twelve miles we walked that day were tiring, we were less tired than we had been on previous days.[1] Looking back, I'm certain

---

[1] We were less tired because we had finally attained some conditioning. We had never taken long-distance walks before and knew nothing about training for a big climb. We were lucky that we had been walking for a week before climbing the Goulet.—Ed.

that part of the reason for our lack of fatigue was not having to talk to people. Except for the family at Mirandol, we hadn't seen a living soul all day. From the top of the mountain, not one sign of human habitation could be discerned for endless miles in all directions.

We reached Le Bleymard around four in the afternoon. We had scrambled easily down the sparsely wooded southern slope of the mountain picking a way through grassy pastures. We finally found a little dirt road at a tiny village called Les Alpiers, and in no time reached the National Highway. As usual, we began to attract attention. A group of young curious girls were the first to stop us. Next a car stopped, and a man started asking us questions. When he heard we planned to walk over the Montagne de la Lozère, he told us we wouldn't be able to do it.

A short way down the highway, a road cut off to Le Bleymard. We had noted on our map there was a very winding dirt road that zigzagged up and over Lozère. This road to Le Bleymard was the start of it. About two hundred yards down the road, we came to a fork. To the left was the road to the village. To the right was the road to the mountain. Standing right at that point was a large sign with the dismal message that the road was closed due to snow.

Considering how pessimistic we had been about lesser problems, I'm at a loss to know why we took all these warnings so lightly. For no reason I can think of we had the attitude that "if you don't look at it, it will go away." But we were going to have a look at it.

Madame Robert had asked us to visit a cousin of hers in Le Bleymard, and we were certainly going to do it. We had few difficulties getting a room in a hotel and a shelter for Modestine. Since it was still light, we took her to a grassy meadow to graze for a while. This gave the children in town a chance to ask "The Questions"[2] and also to speak the few words of English some of them knew. They all seemed to know about Stevenson's *Travels with a Donkey*.

Again in a high mountain village, we found the people quiet and serious. Madame Robert's relatives were most friendly, but completely lacking in gaiety and fun. In fact, most of their conversation was about the hard life in the mountains. They told us the young people left as

---

2 These were the questions put by everybody we met (page 22).—Ed.

soon as they were old enough. Winter in these parts was especially difficult, and they had just been through an unusually severe one. They were very interested in our trip but told us, "You cannot get over the mountain; the road is closed."

We left the door open for failure, but said we were going to try.

At which point the 80-year-old grandmother wrapped herself in a black shawl and said, "I am going to church to pray for you."

On this dismal note we said goodbye and returned to the hotel. We were the only guests at this drab inn. With no one to talk to and nothing to do, we decided on an early dinner.

"Mom, what are we going to do about crossing Mount Lozère?" Roberta asked.

"Well, what do you think I should do?" I countered.

Carol wondered, "Do you think we won't be able to make it?"

Of course, we had heard and seen enough to make our chances seem poor. Not for one second had I considered giving up before we at least tried, so I said, "How about going up there and seeing for ourselves?"

Both girls agreed that we should.

Carol remarked, "Our clothes are all waterproof and warm; what difference does it make if the ground is all covered with snow?"[3]

"What about Modestine's hooves; they might sink in the snow," Roberta mused, "but I agree, we must certainly try."

And that was the last word on the subject for the night.

---

3 I still did not have gloves. Memory fails me as to why I was so confident about facing cold weather again.—Ed.

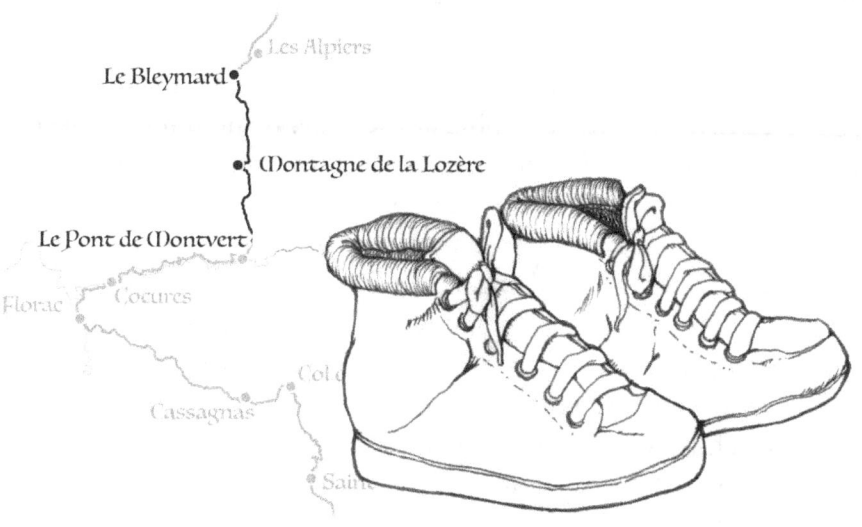

Chapter 11

Path of Stone Pillars

We were up at seven as usual on Monday, 20 May. We dressed, washed, and packed. We ate breakfast. We paid for our room and meals. We brought Modestine to the front of the hotel and loaded her. Before nine we started up the street. We bought laces for Carol's boots. No one paid much attention to us. We left Le Bleymard. Up to now there had been little or no conversation. What was there to say? Our plan for the day was to cross Montagne de la Lozère; that had been the plan ever since April when we had established our schedule. Now we were about to do it, but everyone told us it couldn't be done. Without a satisfactory alternative, we decided to go up there and see what would happen. Actually, each time someone tried to dissuade us, we became more stubborn about trying. Now as we started up the road, we became very determined to do it no matter how tough it was.

The road started going up immediately. We entered a narrow pass, and Le Bleymard was lost to view. The trees on the lower slope were very thick, and our vista was confined to the immediate area through which we were climbing at the time. Although there were a few isolated houses here and there in the beginning, we never saw a single person. We walked without talking. All we could think about was that snow-capped peak we had seen the day before from Montagne de Goulet. The road was fairly steep with few turns; the trees became sparse rather quickly. Suddenly, we found ourselves out of the woods altogether on a bare, brown grassy slope. At the edge of the wood was a chalet used by skiers in the winter. Seeing smoke coming out of the chimney, we tied up Modestine and went over to see if we could have some coffee. Now we would find out for sure what conditions were at the summit.

We were warmly received at the chalet by the couple who lived there. A pot of coffee was hot on the stove. Now we timidly asked what our chances were of going over the top of the mountain. These people, who lived here all the time and had just gone through one of the worst winters on record, didn't know what all the fuss was about. Of course we could reach the top. No, not by the road; it's still closed with tremendous drifts of snow. But you can walk around the drifts. In fact, the road winds around the peak; you can walk in a straight line and get there even faster than you could on the road if it were open. They pointed out the way, and we could see on our map it was a shorter, steeper route. Obviously, the folks in Le Bleymard were right about the road's being closed. They thought no more about it, because nobody walked up there anyway. They really had no way of knowing what the real conditions were. It was just lucky for us that we hadn't been turned away by all the warnings.

Travels with a Donkey had not been written as a guide book for travelers, even though we were using it as such. Most of our trip had been a fairly faithful facsimile of Stevenson's, but there had been certain deviations. Occasionally, we knew we were exactly where Stevenson had been, and this was one of those times. He had described his path to the peak as following a row of stone pillars over a bald turf. We left the road at the chalet, and a couple of hundred yards ahead we reached the first of the giant granite pillars that led us up to the summit. We were certain our feet were following in Stevenson's long-obliterated footsteps. The top of the mountain was bare of all trees. It was a bleak outlook, especially as blue sky had given way to gray. Dozens of swallows were chasing all over the place, but they were the only sign of life.

The day before, we had felt compelled to keep going because we couldn't see the top of the mountain. It was the other way around on the Lozère. We could see the very tip of the peak, the Pic de Finiels, the highest point in the Cévennes, for our entire ascent. Because of the stone pillars, we knew we were on the right path, but we felt the same urge as the day before to push on to the top.

Again, we had become hungry because it was after noon, but still we pushed on. Shortly, a terribly strong wind blew against us. At last, hunger and fatigue got the better of us, and we decided to stop and eat. It was a mighty unpleasant lunch hour. We were freezing cold, and we had to hang on to everything because of the wind.

On the advice of Stevenson, we had bought a bag of oats in Le Bleymard for Modestine. He had seen the top of Lozère from the Goulet, too, and could tell there would be no grass for grazing. We took turns holding a nosebag for Modestine, because it would have been blown away immediately if we had put it down. So far the only snow we had encountered were some tremendous drifts. We could have avoided the snow altogether, but we took a little detour just to see how it felt to walk in it. Except for the wind, the weather had given us no problems. We were surprised, but not disappointed, that all the warnings had been unfounded.

Shortly after lunch, we reached the peak. Once again the northern mountains vanished, and one step further there was a new spectacle in front of us. We could still see mountains stretching range after range, but they had a different appearance. Everything was greener and richer. The wind stopped abruptly, and the balmy Mediterranean climate reached us. It was obvious that at last we had found Spring. The past two days that we had dreaded so much had been accomplished with ease. We were happy enough to sing, and we did.

As Stevenson had written, the pillars ended at the summit. We were not worried since we knew we would find Le Pont-de-Montvert directly south of the peak.

Gleefully, we started down the southern slope of Montagne de la Lozère. We sloshed through meadows soaked with the water of the melting snow, we crossed streams and pastures, and at last we came to the road. We began to return to the world of people, but these were a different kind of people. Broad grins and sunny smiles met us everywhere. We turned down one invitation to have coffee but accepted another. While we sat laughing and talking, Modestine was being spoiled with cookies and sugar. When we arrived in Le Pont-de-Montvert, people were happy to see us and eager to be of assistance. What a contrast with the dour, unsmiling faces in Le Cheylard-l'Évêque or the grim, worried expressions in Le Bleymard.

How we enjoyed that evening in Le Pont-de-Montvert! Stevenson had been interested in its history. He described in some detail the bloody Protestant revolution at the beginning of the eighteenth century and how Le Pont-de-Montvert had become a stronghold of Protestant resistance. We were content to see it as it is today, with the gray stone houses with their red-tiled roofs scattered on each side of the Tarn River. After a delicious dinner, we sat in front of an open fire feeling very pleased with ourselves. For the first time since we left Le Monastier-sur-Gazeille, we were confident we could finish the trip.

Chapter 12

Tea Time

We woke on Tuesday, 21 May, with the music of the Tarn River in our ears. The sun was shining, and the sky was a cloudless blue. The hotel was very comfortable. Scenically, Le Pont-de-Montvert won the prize over any other town we had seen. The people were certainly the most friendly, but we were eager to get an early start and continue the journey. Our condition had been at the opposite extreme in Le Cheylard-l'Évêque, yet we decided to pass the day there. We were really not behaving perversely. At Cheylard, we were thoroughly discouraged by every kind of adversity, and we contemplated other difficulties with the high mountains ahead. This day was different. We knew the worst was over; only four easy days and we would be in Saint Jean-du-Gard. With the finish line in sight, we would not be held back.

After breakfast, we walked to the farm where Modestine had spent the night. Le Pont-de-Montvert is a busy town with people much more in evidence than anywhere else we had been. Because of the milder weather, store fronts were open, people hung out the windows shaking things out and talking to one another, and the ladies made good use of the public outdoor laundry.[1] Everybody talked and smiled as we went by; the word had obviously gone out about us. At the farm were a few more people who had come to look at Modestine.

When I offered to pay the farmer's wife for taking care of our friend, she refused. "Everyone has come to see your donkey; she has brought great honor to our farm."

By nine o'clock we were on our way with fifteen miles to walk before we would reach Florac. The Michelin Tire Company has produced an excellent series of guidebooks on areas of importance for tourists; one of these is entitled *Gorges of the Tarn*. Although the most dramatic reaches of the Tarn River are on the other side of Florac, we knew that this particular area is considered one of the most beautiful in France. The road out of town climbed a few hundred feet and then took a turn that left us able to look down over every part of Le Pont-de-Montvert. Hundreds of artists must have set up an easel at that point to paint the picture. The river, rushing, tumbling, and falling over rocks, is the dramatic central theme. Man's additions, the bridges and houses built with the native gray stone, enlarge the spectacle harmoniously. We were sorry to leave and vowed we would return.

As the Tarn River cuts its canyon directly through high mountains, it was the only route to follow to Florac. Stevenson had said, "A new road leads from Pont de Montvert to Florac by way of the Tarn; a smooth sandy ledge, it runs about halfway between the summit of the cliffs and the river in the bottom of the valley." It was clearly marked on the map, so for once we had no doubt about which way to go. It is a National Highway, paved and marked every hundred meters with a small white stone. Every kilometer is marked with a larger white stone on which is written the distance between towns.

A small village called Saint Laurent-la-Vernède was just past our halfway mark for the day, so we decided to go there for luncheon. Not

---

[1] Throughout France, we saw groups of women in the small towns doing laundry at the public fountains. They pounded wet clothes and sheets against stone slabs. It must have been backbreaking work.—Ed.

even for the purposes of injecting suspense into the story can I think of a thing that worried us that morning.

The river was the main point of our attention. It was never the same at any two points. If it was narrow, the water rushed. If it was wider, the water flowed slowly. Sometimes, in little pools, the water appeared to be standing still. The color of the water varied with each situation. In the broad, slow-moving sections, various shades of blue reflected the sky. When the riverbed was cut into a sharp, narrow V between the cliffs, white foam bubbled over and around the rocks. In occasional waterfalls the water was colorless and transparent until it hit the rocks with a splash. The pools of water were the deepest shades, sometimes brown, but often a rich dark green.

The mountains on each side of the river were covered thickly with trees and shrubs. Often there were slopes yellow with broom. There were many flowers. Stevenson had referred to the chestnut trees; the children or grandchildren of these trees gave some shelter to us, too.

As the morning grew older, it became warmer and warmer. Soon we had removed everything removable; Modestine was piled high with jackets and sweaters. We found it necessary to stop very often; we could see by the kilometer markers that La Vernède was coming closer at a very slow rate. We rationed our water; we had never had to do that before. Towards noon it became unbearably hot. We were very uncomfortable, getting tired, and our feet hurt. The heat had swollen our feet to the point where our shoes felt very tight.[2] With aching feet and the sun beating down on us, we were glad that Modestine couldn't go any faster. We decided that reaching La Vernède for lunch was impossible; instead we would stop at the first place we could find to soak our feet. Many streams fell down the mountain into the Tarn, and by one of these is where we chose to take our break.

The rest didn't do us any good, because we didn't get much rest. The only grass for Modestine was in a narrow strip on the edge of

---

   2 My mother had a congenital overlapping fifth toe deformity on both feet. She believed (perhaps incorrectly) that no medical treatment was possible. She suffered greatly in the pointed-toe high-heeled shoes that were *de rigeur* for middle-class women in the 1950s. Walking always caused her some degree of pain. So when she writes that her feet hurt, the pain must have been excruciating.—Ed.

the road. We couldn't tie her up because there wasn't enough grass in any one place, so we had to take turns holding her rope. There was some shade under the chestnut trees, but by now it was very hot even in the shade. We were very disappointed that our extreme physical discomfort was spoiling what should have been a lovely day. Now all we could think about was getting to Florac as quickly as possible; but, unfortunately, we were still forced to stop over and over again. We finished the last of our water with lunch, planning to refill our bottle at La Vernède. La Vernède became an obsession with us, and we timed ourselves between meter stones, estimating how long it would take us to get there. La Vernède—there it was. A few decrepit houses some hundred yards below the road and a few buildings a hundred yards or so above the road. With seven miles to go before we reached Florac, we were incapable at that point to go a hundred yards or so in the hopes of finding a café or even a well. I don't know how to explain it even now, but we went right on past the village without stopping. We were acting like zombies. We couldn't talk; we had no expressions on our faces. We just kept moving and that was all.

Only a few cars had gone by us all day, but all of a sudden a Jaguar with British license plates came up behind us and stopped.

"I say, there, would you like to have a cup of tea?" came a voice from the car. "We know what you're doing; we have a copy of *Travels with a Donkey* here in the car with us."

This middle-aged British couple had come here for a painting vacation. We were delighted they had chosen just this time and place to do it. We were mystified how they knew they could speak English to us. They evidently had no doubt we were either American or British. Keeping a British stiff upper lip, we didn't let on that a cup of tea would just about save our lives, but we accepted.

The trunk of the Jag was stocked with artist's materials and also the makings of a welcome tea party. I guess when the English travel in foreign parts, they feel it necessary to have emergency equipment for the tea hour. A little stove was quickly lighted and soon the pot of water was boiling hot. We had to supply our own cups, but they had everything else. Not wanting to waste a moment, the lady set up her easel and painted while we drank and chatted.

She asked, "Are you the leader of this group?"

"No," I answered, "I'm Roberta and Carol's mother."

The rest of the conversation on her part was her amazement that a mother and two daughters would be doing such a thing.

It was getting very late, and we regretfully left our friends by the side of the road. I have often wondered how we could ever have gone on if they hadn't come along at that moment. Now it was getting slightly cooler, and soon we arrived at the little village of Cocures, which had a café. We stopped one final time for coffee and were able to go the rest of the way to Florac more comfortably. By this time the girls were tired, but otherwise alright. I was tired. Much worse, my feet were so sore I could hardly walk. All I could think of was sitting down; but, unfortunately, we had to find some place for Modestine and then go to a hotel.

The hotel was no problem; we had passed some hotels on our way to the center of town. Florac was a town of a few thousand people, not a small farm village, so we wondered whether we could find a barn without walking to the outskirts. I asked a young man if he knew of someone who could care for Modestine. He didn't. Neither did anyone else. Then someone suggested we inquire at a certain butcher shop.

All of this was taking a long time. My feet were giving me much pain. All of a sudden I looked at Modestine, and she seemed to be on the verge of collapse. She had appeared to have suffered quite a bit during the heat of the day. It had been an agonizing fifteen miles from Le Pont-de-Montvert for her as well as for us. I felt very sorry for her and decided she had had enough for one day. We removed the fifty-pound load from her back, and I put it on mine. That didn't relieve my feet any, but at least I felt better about our faithful little animal.

We found the butcher, waited while some customers were attended to, and read the sign on the wall: "Sausages: specialty of the house." We recalled the "joke" many people had made when they saw Modestine. "You should make sausage out of her!" We wondered whether the same idea would occur to the butcher.

Sausages or not, the butcher had a barn and was willing to feed and house Modestine. Loaded down under the packs, we walked Modestine to her hotel and then found one for ourselves.

As Florac is a tourist center of renown, we found a truly excellent hotel. It was so excellent with its carpets on the floor and crystal chandeliers in the dining room that we looked like tramps in our dirty hiking outfits. We were given very cool treatment at the front desk and then shown up to small plain rooms on the fourth floor. I wouldn't have minded any of that if I hadn't had the burden of the packs and my aching feet. The hotel's pain of accepting such disreputable guests was nothing compared to mine.

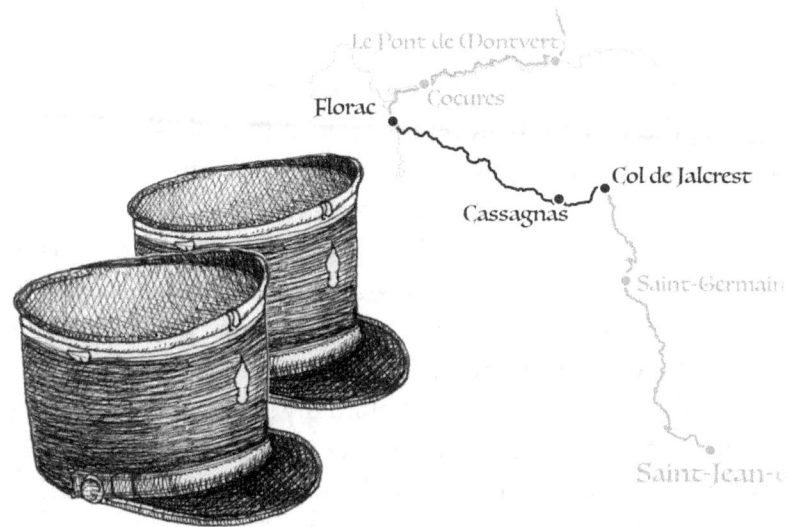

Chapter 13

Stopped by Gendarmes

Each day of the trip had a personality all of its own. We had good days and bad days. Whether a day was good or bad depended on many factors, but I think weather was the most important one.[1] The extreme cold on our way to Le Cheylard-l'Évêque and the extreme heat between Le Pont-de-Montvert and Florac made these very bad days. This day, Wednesday, 22 May, was to be a very good one, because the weather, especially by contrast with the previous one, was comfortable for walking. We woke to see a gray sky. It was cool, but not cold; drizzly, but not too wet.

We couldn't wait to get through breakfast and fetch Modestine to see if she was still alive. Finding that she was not a sausage, the girls loaded the packs on her while I settled our bill at the hotel. The same cool young lady was at the desk, still not convinced we had been

---

[1] Stevenson's frame of mind on his walk was also greatly influenced by the weather.—Ed.

respectable guests. Seldom did I break our rigid code of behavior concerning the way we believed American tourists should conduct themselves. Realizing foreigners think that all Americans are millionaires and that this causes widespread resentment towards us, we were always careful about any show of what might be construed as wealth. However, in case this snippy clerk had doubted our ability to pay this 53.95 franc ($10.85) bill, I spread all three of my checkbooks out on the counter. Actually, each book contained traveler's checks of different denominations, and I habitually selected one or the other depending on the present need, but I never exhibited them in a lavish display. Perhaps if this young lady had not responded to this uncalled-for crudeness of mine, I wouldn't be telling this unlovely story about myself. Quite the contrary was true, as she fell all over herself with politeness and respect for the first time. Actually, I felt ashamed of myself; it was none of my business to teach her a lesson. I left to join the girls outside and tell them what had just happened. The story was a little sick, but it was funny, too.

Before we left Florac, we went to a shoe store to buy a couple of hard-soled felt slippers for me. They are the customary footwear of all the peasant women in France. I decided to buy these unsightly things, in case there was any future need of them.

We didn't leave Florac until almost ten. We were sorry to get a late start because we had fifteen miles to go that day. We were heading for Col de Jalcrest. Stevenson had followed the Mimente River out of Florac as far as a town called Cassagnas. Then he left the river and cut over a mountain directly southeast to Saint-Germain-de-Calberte. We were advised by all and sundry to continue past Cassagnas to the pass; it was impossible to do it any other way. Whether it was or wasn't we'll never know, because we accepted the advice, remembering our detour on the way to Le Cheylard-l'Évêque where the warning had been true.[2]

The narrow, winding valley of the Mimente is not the same spectacle as the gorges of the Tarn River, yet this sparkling little stream is a happy sight to see. Rugged mountains frame its banks both to the

---

2   Yet the warnings had been false for crossing the Montagne de la Lozère.—Ed.

north and the south. The valley is never wide, but occasionally we saw grassy meadows full of every spring flower in full bloom. During our walk we crossed the river on little bridges time and again. In addition to the road, there was a single-track railroad that often disappeared into tunnels through the mountains. Depending on the width of the valley at any point, the road, the river, and the tracks played hide and seek with one other. Sometimes we could see one or the other, sometimes neither. There was nothing particularly noteworthy all day, but we enjoyed looking at any of these features that attracted our attention. We felt good, not suffering from heat, cold, thirst, or any other discomforts—quite a change from the day before.

Although the road was a two-lane paved National Highway, there was very little traffic. The few towns along the way were never directly on the road, so we were not fatigued by many long explanations in French about what we were doing. At one point a VW bus passed us and disappeared around a curve.

"An American!" Carol shouted, recognizing the white oval plates with the black printing that are the German plates on cars sold for export. We had found these cars, so licensed, were almost invariably owned by Americans.

"I wonder why she didn't stop?" Roberta said, because seldom did a car ever pass without at least slowing down to get a better look at us. Before we could think any more about it, we were suddenly confronted with the driver of the VW, running towards us with a movie camera whirring away in our direction.

"Hello!" I called, and that poor woman almost fell off the edge of the road in surprise.

"Are you American?" she asked in amazement. Then, "What are you doing here?"

I told her.

She said, "Aren't you scared walking around these mountains? I came here with a copy of *Travels with a Donkey* to see how many of these places I could drive to in a car. I keep my windows rolled up and my doors locked, but I've seen enough. I'm leaving now."

She was a middle-aged woman from Akron, Ohio, traveling in Europe on her vacation. Although single, she had bought a wedding ring for some kind of protection. It was clear these wild parts were not for her:

"I think you're the bravest people I've ever met," she said.

We felt very sorry for her. It would have been nice to see the colored movies she had taken of us, but somehow we never thought to ask her name.[3]

To add to the ease of the whole day, we reached a small town with a café right on the road just as we were getting hungry. Fortunately, there was a convenient tree to which to tie Modestine in the middle of a patch of grass. The pieces of the day were fitting together perfectly. There was even a clean, well-operating toilet in the café, a phenomenon always worthy of comment and commendation.

In the middle of the afternoon, a car came along, slowing down sufficiently before it reached us, and stopped alongside.

The driver turned off the motor and began to speak to us in a very deliberate fashion, "I am Madame Pantel, and I live in Saint-Germain-de-Calberte where you will be tomorrow. I read about you in the newspaper, and I have been watching for you. When you come to Saint Germain, come to my house and I will help you get settled for the night."

"Now that is very pleasant to look forward to," I told her. "Thank you very much."

"I won't delay you anymore. See you tomorrow." She drove off.

When we were about three miles from Col de Jalcrest, it started to rain quite hard. We hoped Modestine didn't mind, because we certainly didn't. The air felt so cool and fresh, it was exhilarating. It was just what we needed to revive us after walking so many miles. Then came the one and only sour note of the day. Two gendarmes drove up, stopped their car, and came running over to us.

"*Les cartes d'identité!*" ("Passports!") they demanded brusquely.

I looked at them in amazement, thinking they must certainly be kidding. I gave a quick glance at my two drenched young daughters and the tiny soaking wet donkey. Did they really think we were suspi-

---

3 I've often wondered about this incident. If she thought we were French and that the French were dangerous, why did she risk provoking us by filming us first and asking questions later?—Ed.

cious characters? For the second time that day, I did not behave in a manner suitable to Americans traveling abroad.

"We are American citizens. These are my daughters. I cannot take my passport out in this pouring down rain. If you will go to the hotel in Col de Jalcrest and wait for us, I will show you our passports then."

I was very surprised they agreed to this.

"We will see you at the hotel," they shouted.

We thought the whole thing was very funny but on the outrageous side, too.

We reached the pass and the hotel shortly after that little encounter. A man was standing by the road as we arrived, and I asked him the usual nightly question: "Do you know someone who has room for our donkey?"

Recalling the misery I suffered the previous night in Florac solving this problem, I was almost afraid to hear his answer.

There was no doubt that this was one of our Good Days when he replied, "I have, Madame, and that is my house right there," pointing across the street.

The girls took our baggage into the hotel, and I escorted our wet little lady into one of the nicest lodgings she had. It was full of hay, and the farmer said he would bring her water and then brush her coat.

The hotel was adequate. It seemed to be a popular meeting place for the neighborhood, because the lobby was full of people, including, of course, our gendarmes.

After getting out of our wet overclothes, I went over to them and asked them sweetly, "Would you like to see our passports now?"

Everyone was watching us and they looked embarrassed.

"Oh, no, Madame!" was the only graceful out for them under the circumstances.

I made myself at home in my new, extremely ugly slippers. We enjoyed a good dinner. I talked to some of the people in the hotel while Roberta and Carol played with three adorable kittens. That was a good day.

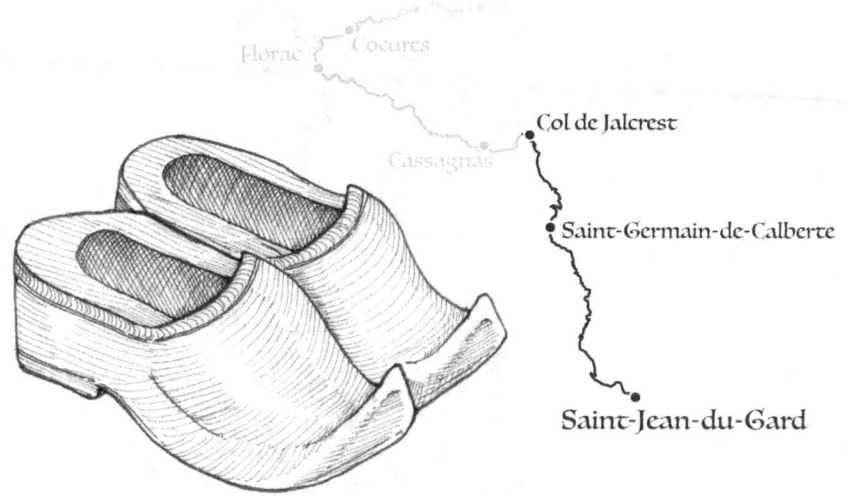

Chapter 14

Journey's End

We were awakened at seven (Thursday, 23 May) and immediately ran to the window to see if the rain had stopped. It was quite foggy, but pieces of blue sky and sun were beginning to win out over the mist. After breakfast we checked out of the hotel and took our packs onto the front porch. All three of us went for Modestine, who as usual was neither happy nor unhappy about seeing us. The farmer's family was all out watching us lead her from the barn. The farmer gave her a last going-over with a stiff brush, and his wife painted her various scratches with gentian violet.[1] They refused to take a franc from us for all their care.

A solid wall of mountain had loomed overhead to the south from Florac to Col de Jalcrest. At Col de Jalcrest, a tremendous pass opened up. From the top of the pass, the view was magnificent, mile after mile of mountains rising to the east and the west of a narrow valley. It was

---

1 Gentian violet is an antiseptic liquid.—Ed.

Figure 8. Modestine and Carol

only a ten-mile hike to Saint Germain-de-Calberte, where we would spend the night. It was sunny, but cool as we followed the narrow, winding road down the pass. The slopes were entirely covered with trees; none of this particular area was good enough even for grazing. Occasionally, we would see the house of a chestnut farmer, but there were no villages. To us that meant no coffee before Saint Germain.

We occupied ourselves by timing the distance between kilometer stones. We were used to flying by one every minute in the car; Modestine's pace was four per hour. As we were patiently counting off each set of ten one-hundred-meter stones to each kilometer, we passed a house. We were more than content to stop counting stones and accept an invitation for a cup of coffee. I assume we always looked thirsty; coffee, tea, wine, and endless aperitifs had come our way for over one hundred miles.

One of the numerous citizens on hand to welcome us to Saint Germain-de-Calberte was Madame Alice Pantel, who had spoken to us on the road the day before. She graciously helped us make the usual arrangements for Modestine and ourselves and then invited us to tea. She was anxious to have us meet the pastor, who could speak to us in English. In due time the pastor came, but he spoke to us in French. It appeared he shared the sentiment of many others we had met, "When in France, one must speak French." And so we did.

It was a long and difficult fifteen miles from Saint Germain-de-Calberte to Saint Jean-du-Gard. We hesitated before we left the road to follow Stevenson's route straight up and over Montagne Saint-Pierre. Although it was not clear enough to be able to see the Mediterranean Sea from the summit, it was a satisfaction to realize it was so near.

We became very quiet as we descended our last mountain and hiked the final miles. Then, at last, we had arrived: Saint Jean-du-Gard! Thirteen days and one hundred thirty-five miles. We were happy and very proud of our achievement.[2]

---

    2 Towards the end of Stevenson's book, he appears to be running out of things to say, and the same may have happened to my mother. I recall that final day walking into Saint Jean-du-Gard as wonderfully happy.—Ed.

Chapter 15

Farewells

We spent a full day (Saturday, 25 May 1963) in Saint Jean-du-Gard trying to find a suitable arrangement to send Modestine to the Hellendorns. The mayor and the president of the Syndicat d'initiative came to see us. A charming couple, who gave us lunch at their home, took us in tow and helped us find someone who would drive us and Modestine to Langogne. It wasn't until after five in the afternoon that we found a man who was licensed to carry animals in his truck. We agreed on a price and arranged to meet him at four o'clock the following morning.

At seven thirty on Sunday morning, we presented Modestine to Nanette and Rombout. We were relieved to be able to leave her in good hands. We had come to love our little donkey. She had given us some anxious moments in the early days but had finally become a completely satisfactory beast of burden. We loved her curious habits. She was desperately afraid of water and would shy at even the tiniest puddle in the road. She would shy at shiny tar that looked wet. It was

Figure 9. Betty, Modestine, and Carol

an amazing sight to see her little burdened body leap over a stream. We admired her stamina on the long hard days. Because she behaved so valiantly, we babied and spoiled her in every way. Her nose was usually stained with lipstick from many well-deserved kisses. She loved to share our lunch with us and expected to be hand fed. Although we knew the Hellendorns would have little time to spoil her, we were sure they would treat her well.

On Monday, 27 May 1963, we said goodbye to the Hellendorns after another night sleeping in their barn. We said goodbye to our dear Modestine and hoped to see her again someday. Then we returned for a final two days in Le Monastier-sur-Gazeille.

Our story is not the same as Robert Louis Stevenson's, and it does not have to be. Our memories are our own. The incredible contrasts in our living arrangements: one night in a pleasant hotel, the next night in a barn. The splendor of spring in the magnificent Cévennes mountains. But over and above every other memory is the goodness and kindness of the people. Strangers who became friends.

Friends whose love accompanied us on each of the one hundred thirty-five miles from Le Monastier to Saint Jean-du-Gard.

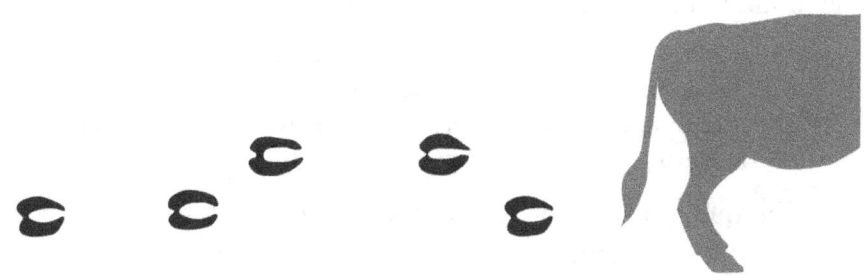

Afterword

My mother's manuscript concludes in May 1963. It was unclear when, if ever, we would return to the Cévennes. Her next visit occurred in 1965 when she drove me and a couple of my friends from school during our spring vacation. We spent several days in Le Monastier-sur-Gazeille during which Betty hatched a plan to donate a monument celebrating the beginning of Robert Louis Stevenson's 1878 journey.

THE MONUMENT

In 1963 we noticed Le Monastier did not have a marker to acknowledge that a well-known author had once stayed there and written about the town. We doubted this lack stemmed from any hostility towards Stevenson—the idea of raising a monument had probably never occurred to anybody. It occurred to Betty. She offered to pay for installing a small *stèle* (plinth). I wasn't present at its dedication, but I've reconstructed the events as best I can from scattered documents and my mother's letters.

She returned to Le Monastier in June 1965 with the goal of donating a monument to Stevenson as a gesture of thanks to all the people who were so good to us in 1963. She saw an opportunity for the monument's dedication to attract publicity. She wrote:

> The syndicat d'initiative is forever looking for ways to attract people here. In perhaps almost too American fashion I drew a picture for them of an event which, if well enough done, could reach the notice of the international press.

She thought there were two key ingredients for success: (1) to have someone from Edinburgh at the dedication to represent Stevenson and (2) to get coverage from French television. She wasn't sure how to make contact with the appropriate person in Edinburgh, but got an idea from Dr. Ollier. Once he had corresponded with the City Librarian of Edinburgh, so she wrote to the librarian, asking about people connected with Stevenson.

*D'ici partit
le 22 Septembre 1878
Robert Louis Stevenson pour son voyage
a travers les Cévennes avec un âne.*

(This is the place from which
Robert Louis Stevenson
departed on the
22 September 1878
for his travels across the Cévennes
with a donkey.)

Figure 10. The plinth and its inscription

Figure 11. Syndicat d'Initiative

It was easier than I had anticipated. One ancient cousin, Alan Stevenson, couldn't have cared less, but he sent me to another cousin, Nancy Brackett. What a treasure! President of the RLS Society, her grandmother and Stevenson's mother were first cousins, but more important charming, honored and delighted to have been asked, and able to pay her own way.

Betty appears to have stayed in Le Monastier for a few weeks, during which she ordered a plaque with the agreement of the Syndicat d'Initiative. They set the date of Saturday, 2 October, for the dedication of the monument in the Place Saint-Jean. I do not know who composed the inscription, but I suspect it was Dr. Ollier. Betty's name does not appear on either the plaque or the associated plinth.

Betty left France for England at the end of June to spend the school vacation with me. We traveled in England and Scotland. After I returned to school, she met Madame Robert in London, and they went back to France together.

She continues:

> I went personally to every conceivable newspaper and news service in Edinburgh, London, and Paris. Madame Robert was with me that day in Paris and is still telling anyone who will listen to her how we raced from The New York Times to the New York Tribune to the Associated Press and then Time-Life.

The two of them returned to Le Monastier on Tuesday, 28 September.

> Then the real fun started! With one single exception, nothing had been done to prepare for Saturday. The one exception was the sending of the official invitations by the S.I. and it might have been better if that had not been done. Before doing anything that evening, we drove to the Place St. Jean to see the monument. The Place was a filthy, littered mess and there was no monument! Without even eating we went right over to M. Chalindar's to see what was up. Gad.

Apparently, the Conseil Municipal—the town council—had decided that everything in the Place Saint Jean was to be rearranged, and special plans were required before any monument could be erected. There was already a plan in force for the square in front of the post office, but no work had begun.

> Don't ask me how, but on Wednesday night at a special meeting, it was decided to plant trees, build sidewalks, place benches AND the monument in that Place. In the future, the monument will be moved to the Place St. Jean. But the absolutely astonishing phenomenon was the complete renovation of the Place de la Poste in two-and-a-half days. At noon on Sat, the plaque was put in place.[1]

> Wednesday night both the Conseil Municipal and the S.I. held meetings. Major item of agenda for each was the dedication three days later. Thursday work on the Place began, M. Chalindar got around to talking to the TV folks, he wrote some articles for the local papers, someone starting looking around in Le Puy for American and British flags, Mme. Robert was here, there and everywhere hunting down and borrowing old costumes and taking them to a couterière for repairs. A loud speaker system was ordered. Etc. Etc. I never saw anything like it in Le Monastier before. Friday morning Mme. Robert and I set off for Lyon to meet Mrs. Brackett at the airport. We were absolutely certain in our minds that finally everything was being done, and we spent a very peaceful day. We returned here with Mrs. Brackett and the plan was for me to have a quick bite and then go down to the office of the S.I. to help Mme. Robert decorate.

> When I got down there it was locked and dark. I went over to M. Chalindar's and were the sparks ever flying! The Conseil Municipal had in

---

1 I do not believe the monument has ever been moved.—Ed.

a body taken exception to the wording in the S.I.'s invitation (to this day neither Mme. Robert or I have ever been able to find a copy of this offensive letter); they decided that the S.I. wanted to run Le Monastier and as for them, they would have nothing further to do with the dedication. In countless newspapers the following morning everyone was going to read that the Conseil Municipal would offer a *vin d'honneur* at the Mairie, but it just wasn't going to be. What an uproar! We marched over to tell this great news to Dr. Ollier. If ever there was a man who did not want to take over running a town, it is certainly Dr. Ollier. Now what to do? Of course we must see the maire. Poor, dear, sweet M. Convers. Throughout he looked like he wished he were anywhere else. Being a member of both groups and tituarly the most influential, it was up to him to patch things up. I put in my two bits and said that Roberta, Carol, and I do not think about either the the S.I. or the Conseil Municipal. We simply think of Le Monastier. Furthermore, in years to come the English and Americans who find their way here would feel the same. M. Convers said very little; of course he could promise nothing, but he did agree to hold an emergency meeting of the Conseil at noon SATURDAY!

The politics of a small town can be impenetrable by an outsider. Perhaps a faction was offended by this American woman and her ideas, or it might have had nothing to do with her. Whatever the provocation, in the end, the Conseil agreed to offer the *vin d'honneur* (reception).

And so all the pieces fell into place. I can't begin to describe the hysterical activities just before the dedication. One of Mme. Robert's last problems was convincing the school authorities to release the children early for the parade. My only repose all day was the hour I spent at the coiffeuse followed then by a hasty lunch and a mad dash into Le Puy to get the costumes from the couturier and transport some girls back here. When I arrived at Mme. Robert's at 2:00; what a scene. The donkey [not Modestine] was eating up the flowers in the garden and Jean-Pierre was getting acquainted with it.

After the last-minute rush to dress the childen, it was time for the festivities to begin.

The whole town was decorated with flags. On each public building was placed a freshly painted plaque with the letters: RF [Republic Francais] in gold and the French, American, and British flags flying together. Shortly after 3:00 in the afternoon, Nancy and I drove to the lace-and-

Figure 12. Betty, unknown dignitary, Nancy Brackett, and Dr. Ollier giving speech at dedication of monument

flower-decorated office of the Syndicat d'Initiative for the start of 12 solid hours of celebration. Gathered there were all the members of the S.I., the members of the Conseil Municipal, various dignitaries, invited guests, and the two of us. The most touching part of the whole day for me was the presence of M. Galière; he is now old and ill, but he came anyway.[2] Shortly after 3:30 we could hear the band approaching, and we all trooped out to the street. What a procession! First the wonderful little drum and bugle corps; la Clique Saint-Chaffre led by the mailman "Tintin" Breysse. Next Jean-Pierre Vaggiani dressed up as Stevenson and leading a donkey. Next 7 girls and 7 boys dressed in the authentic clothes of the 19th century right down to their sabots. And finally all the school children from all four of the schools who were dismissed early for this great occasion.

After the band played a number for us, we all joined the procession and proceeded to the Place. What a crowd had assembled there! In addition

---

2 M. Galière is the owner of the Hôtel des Pins in La Bastide where we stayed because women were not allowed to sleep at Our Lady of the Snows.—Ed.

Following Robert Louis Stevenson with a Donkey 109

Figure 13. Betty, Nancy Brackett, and unknown dignitary at the monument

to what looked like everyone in town, there were hordes of reporters, photographers, French national television and various odds and ends of spectators like the little French lady who is a professor of English at the university of Aix-en-Provence.

As soon as the whole procession had arrived at the flower and flag bedecked Place, the band sounded a mighty fanfare and the ceremony

Figure 14. Betty and procession after the dedication of the monument

started. First Dr. Ollier gave a beautiful speech; most scholarly done, on the history of the connection between Stevenson and Le Monastier. Then the Maire gave another excellent speech starting with the first sentence of *"Travels with a Donkey"*; *"Dans une petite localité nommée Le Monastier, sis en une agréable vallée de montagnes, à 15 mile du Puy, j'ai passé un mois de journées délicieuses."*[3] And he continued by recalling our very first visit when, painstakingly with a dictionary, we made the first steps in preparing for our own "travels with a donkey".

During the planning, Betty had requested that she be excused from making a speech, saying that her actions were more important than her words. Did she feel she was already receiving too much atten-

---

3 This is the first line of *Travels with a Donkey* translated into French: "In a little place called Le Monastier, in a pleasant highland valley fifteen miles from Le Puy, I spent about a month of fine days."—Ed.

tion? Did she lack confidence in her ability to write and deliver the expected French rhetorical flourishes? Whatever the reason, she did not stand at the microphone.

> Nancy Brackett then said a few words. Next there was another fanfare and Nancy and I unveiled the monument. It was a most solemn moment. Next blaring over the P.A. came the anthems of our three countries. And finally Nancy and I were presented with huge bouquets of flowers by the children. The great procession then regrouped and once again led by la Clique Saint-Chaffre we paraded through the town.

The next item on the agenda was that *cause celebre:* the vin d'honneur at the *Mairie.*

> A long table draped in white was set up replete with champagne glasses in what had been, many centuries ago, the main building of the monastery. The glasses were filled and M. Convers on behalf of the Conseil Municipal proposed the toast to Roberta, Carol and Betty Gladstone, *citoyennes d'honneur du Monastier!* Various other toasts followed. Nancy presented a bouquet of heather, picked by the former home of Stevenson and also a handsome framed bronze medallion of Stevenson. The first to the Conseil Municipal and the second to the Syndicat d'Initiative. Thus ended the formal aspects of the day.

But no celebration would be complete without a dinner. The Syndicat d'Initiative put on a sumptuous formal banquet at a local hotel. Betty noted how her presence as an American brought down the class barriers:

> Mme. Ollier will never in her life get over the fact that she danced with M. Chalindar and also her housepainter who had danced with her maid the week before! There was incessant moving about, singing and dancing (to an accordion). Who kissed whom in any case can never be a matter of record, because, with the possible exception of Mme. Ollier, no one remembers.

Betty got her wish of publicity for Le Monastier, including an article from the Associated Press wire service:

> "The Scotsman" in Edinburgh and "Figaro" in Paris printed articles. The Associated Press item was at least on the front page of the S.F. Chronicle. I will wonder all my life how many American papers chose to print that little item. I have lost count of all the items in the local regional papers around here. It was televised. And already if you please,

Figure 15. Jean-Pierre Vaggiani getting acquainted with his donkey

this week a young English girl teaching in St. Etienne arrived here as a result of reading the story.

Everyone in Le Monastier is completely satisfied that it all went as it did.

Farewell to Le Monastier

After the dedication Betty traveled some more before renting an apartment in Le Monastier. She stayed there for the next two years.

Figure 16. Jean-Pierre Vaggiani and his donkey reach a meeting of minds

She and Madame Robert became close friends. My sister and I visited several times. I remember happy afternoons in Madame Robert's sitting room watching her crochet at the speed of light. She taught all of us how to do needlepoint. Betty and Roberta became fluent in French, although I remained tongue tied.

Once all three of us were in Le Monastier at Christmas time. I grew very tired of hearing *Il est né, le divin enfant* (He is born, the heavenly child). I was invited to a party of the town's teenagers, who were very friendly to me. We danced to the French version of "Yellow Submarine," which became a "green submarine." We joined the large gathering in the church on Christmas Eve for midnight mass when suddenly all the lights went out. After some candlelit confusion, we realized that because almost everyone was there, "everyone" included the town electrician, who was able to put things to rights.

We had Christmas dinner with Dr. Ollier's family—the only time I've ever eaten in a private house with a maid to prepare the food and

Figure 17. Nancy Brackett, Dr. Ollier, and Betty at the *vin d'honneur*

Figure 18. Madame Ollier, unknown man, Nancy Brackett, unknown man, Betty, and Dr. Ollier at the banquet

Following Robert Louis Stevenson with a Donkey 115

Figure 19. Press coverage of the monument dedication

bring it up from the kitchen. The Ollier sons were distressed by how my sister and I buttered the whole slice of bread before eating it; that was not *comme il faut* (correct etiquette). They showed us the "correct" way to eat bread: tear off a piece for a mouthful and butter just that piece before eating it.

In January after that Christmas, Betty gave a Twelfth Night party that was also a housewarming for her new apartment. The French term for "housewarming" is "hang the fire chain," an expression that presumably dates from the time when cooking was done over an open fire with pots hanging from the chimney by a chain. Betty found an old fire chain at an antique store and asked a blacksmith to open the links so she had a stack of individual iron rings. She painted each link with gold paint and included one in each invitation she sent out asking each person to come and "hang our fire chain." Everybody was astonished that she would think of such a thing and said *"Tres original!"* We had a "Three Kings" cake, which in America is associated with New Orleans and Mardi Gras instead of Epiphany. There was lots of champagne and lively conversation of which I understood practically nothing.

Eventually, Betty moved to England, where she met her second husband who was a journalist. He also spoke French and loved France, so they visited Le Monastier every year until 1979 when they decided to retire in Santa Fe, New Mexico.

Madame Robert visited Betty and her husband in Santa Fe, as did some of the younger generation of Betty's French friends. Betty died in Santa Fe in 1990 at the age of seventy-one. Her final mention in the newspapers of the Cévennes was an obituary written by Madame Robert.

> "Hello Betty!" This friendly and joyful greeting that adults and children alike gave to an American woman from California, who came here in 1963 to follow R. L. Stevenson's footsteps, won't be heard again. Betty is gone, the victim of inoperable lung cancer.
>
> Everyone who knew and loved her should know what she wrote in her letter giving me the tragic news: "Tell my friends that the years I spent in Le Monastier were some of the happiest in my life."

Figure 20. Betty in Le Monastier in 1963—the picture that appeared in her French obituary

Those of you who did not know her will find concrete evidence of her stay. She donated the monument in the post office square commemorating Stevenson's departure point. She helped obtain a gift from the Society of Friends of R. L. Stevenson in Edinburgh which allowed us to commission the paintings in the town hall of the stages of Stevenson's trip. The artist was a talented friend of Betty's; Jean de la Fontinelle.

She moved heaven and earth to make our little corner of France better known, and many others in their turn have made the trek from Le Monastier to St Jean du Gard.

And so once again I say, with all of you, "Hello, Betty, our friend."

Further Reading

Bernstein, Jeremy. "A Reporter at Large: Travels with Jaccoux in the Cevennes." *The New Yorker* (August 12, 1985): 70–81.

Castle, Alan. *The Robert Louis Stevenson Trail: A Walking Tour in the Velay and Cévennes, Southern France.* Milnthorpe, United Kingdom: Cicerone Press, 1992.

Holmes, Richard. *Footsteps: Adventures of a Romantic Biographer.* New York: Viking, Elisabeth Sifton Books, 1985.

Macaskill, Hilary, and Molly Wood. *Downhill All The Way: Walking with Donkeys on the Stevenson Trail—Travels in the Cévennes.* London: Frances Lincoln Limited, 2006.

Nicholson, Adam. *Long Walks in France.* New York: Harmony Books, 1983.

Ress, Paul. *Shaggy Dog Tales: 58 1/2 Years of Reportage.* Bloomington, Indiana: Xlibris, 2006.

Stevenson, Robert Louis. *Travels with a Donkey in the Cévennes.* London: C. Keegan Paul & Co., 1879.

Index

A

L'Abbaye Notre Dame des Neiges 60, 63, 68
Abbé, Le Monastier sur Gazeille 17, 19
L'Academie française 1
Acquino, Eric 62
Akron, Ohio 91
  woman from 91, 92
Allier River 40, 51, 58, 59, 68
America 116
les Americaines 38, 40
American xii, 2, 4, 9, 10, 15, 17, 35, 38, 41, 45, 55, 63, 86, 90, 91, 93, 104, 106, 107, 111, 116
Americas 25
Amsterdam 44
animals 54, 99
  bear 76
  chickens 44
  cows 18, 28, 44, 47, 54, 61
  dog 18, 28, 52
  donkey i, iii, v, xi, 1, 2, 3, 4, 5, 6, 7, 9, 10, 11, 12, 13, 15, 16, 17, 19, 20, 21, 22, 23, 25, 26, 29, 35, 36, 39, 41, 42, 45, 51, 58, 59, 60, 62, 63, 65, 67, 84, 91, 92, 93, 99, 104, 110, 119
  donkey, Jean-Pierre Vaggiani's 107, 108, 112, 113
  geese 44
  goats 44, 54
  horse 17
  kittens 93
  mouse 18
  oxen 60
  rabbits 44
  sheep 54
  swallows 81
  wolves 15
aperitifs 14, 24, 38, 97
Argos 62
Armargiers 35

Associated Press 105, 111
Athens 4
Australian 16
automobiles
    Citroën 2CV 10, 17
    Jaguar 86
    Jeep 63
    VW bus 91

B

barn 2, 18, 19, 29, 43, 44, 47, 48, 49, 50, 52, 53, 54, 55, 59, 61, 62, 87, 95, 100, 101
    L'Abbaye Notre Dame des Neiges 61
    Le Monastier-sur-Gazeille 18, 19
Barret farm 48, 49
La Bastide-Puylaurent 60, 61, 62, 65, 69, 108
bear 76
Beaufort Castle. *See* Château de Beaufort
Berkeley, California xii
blacksmith 116
Le Bleymard 74, 76, 77, 79, 80, 81, 82
Bonhomme, Alphonse 14
Le Bouchet-Saint-Nicholas 21, 23, 24, 25, 28, 29, 33, 34, 35, 38
Brackett, Nancy 105, 106, 108, 109, 111, 114
Brazil 62
Breysse, "Tintin" 108
British 16, 86, 106, 107
British couple 86
butcher 87

C

cabinet 54
café 20, 35, 39, 50, 52, 53, 54, 55, 59, 86, 87, 92
California xii, 35, 116
Cassagnas 90
Cévennes xi, xii, 1, 2, 5, 12, 15, 17, 22, 30, 35, 57, 58, 60, 61, 62, 69, 73, 74, 81, 101, 103, 104, 116, 119
Chalindar, Monsieur 14, 20, 106, 111
Le Chambon-sur-Lignon 3, 4, 35
champagne 20, 111, 116
Chamson, Andre 1
Charbonnières-les-Bains 34
Charre, Monsieur Ernest 18, 19, 20
Chasseradès 68, 69, 73, 74, 75
Le Chassezac River 74
Château de Beaufort 24
Le Cheylard-l'Évêque 48, 49, 50, 51, 53, 55, 57, 58, 59, 62, 63, 69, 71, 82, 83, 89, 90
Le Cheylard l'Evêque café family 52
    Josette 52, 53, 55, 57
    Madame 52, 53, 55, 56
    Monsieur 52, 53, 54
chickens 44
church 17, 18, 19, 24, 113
la Clique Saint-Chaffre 108, 111
clothing and equipment 5, 6, 7, 21
Cocures 87
coffee 23, 35, 36, 44, 47, 50, 53, 55, 60, 62, 80, 82, 87, 96, 97
cold 6, 30, 37, 40, 49, 51, 52, 53, 54, 56, 69, 78, 81, 89, 91
Col de Jalcrest 90, 92, 93, 95
    farmer's family 95
Conseil Municipal 106, 107, 108, 111
Convers
    Françoise 24
    Madame 12, 14, 15
    Monsier, Mayor of Le Monastier-sur-Gazeille 3, 12, 13, 14, 16, 24, 29, 35, 107, 110, 111
    Roland 24
Cooper, Gordon
    astronaut 59
Costoros 26, 27
Côte d'Azur 57
countries
    Americas 25
    Brazil 62

England xii, 2, 17, 105, 116
France xi, xii, 1, 2, 9, 10, 30, 37, 44, 50, 84, 90, 97, 105, 116, 117, 119
Germany 30
Greece 2, 62
Holland 44, 45
Italy 6
Scotland 105
Spain 6, 30
United States xii, 9, 14, 15, 40, 55, 59
cows 18, 28, 44, 47, 54, 61
croissants 9

D

dedication of Stevenson monument xii, 103, 104, 105, 106, 107, 108, 110, 112, 115
Delphi 62
dictionary 3
dog 18, 28, 52
donkey i, iii, v, xi, 1, 2, 3, 4, 5, 6, 7, 9, 10, 11, 12, 13, 15, 16, 17, 19, 20, 21, 22, 23, 25, 26, 29, 35, 36, 39, 41, 42, 45, 51, 58, 59, 60, 62, 63, 65, 67, 84, 91, 92, 93, 99, 104, 110, 119
donkey, Jean-Pierre Vaggiani's 107, 108, 112, 113
Dutch 39, 41, 44
Dutchman 41

E

Edinburgh 104, 105, 111, 117
    City Librarian 104
England xii, 2, 17, 105, 116
English
    language 25, 34, 41, 42, 44, 67, 71, 77, 86, 97, 109
    of England 16, 86, 107, 112
Eric Acquino 62
L'Estampe 74
Europe xii, 2, 9, 24, 30, 35, 39, 42, 47, 53, 91

F

farm 10, 36, 37, 42, 43, 44, 47, 49, 83, 84, 87
    Barret 48, 49
farmer 10, 15, 28, 29, 33, 36, 39, 41, 43, 49, 93, 95, 96
farmers 36, 44
farmer's family
    Col de Jalcrest 95
farmer's wife
    Le Pont-de-Montvert 84
farrier 42, 43
Faure, Antonin 14
Fay sur Lignon 5, 15
fencing 25
Florac 84, 86, 87, 88, 89, 90, 93, 95
de la Fontinelle, Jean 117
Fouzilhic and Fouzilhac 48, 49
France xi, xii, 1, 2, 9, 10, 30, 37, 44, 84, 90, 97, 105, 116, 117, 119
French xii, 3, 4, 9, 13, 29
    language 16, 23, 29, 36, 37, 42, 50, 91, 97, 113, 116, 117
    of France 24, 29, 41, 42, 44, 50, 92, 104, 116

G

gale 50
Galière, Monsieur 60, 61, 62, 63, 68, 108
gas station 47
Gazeille River 11, 22
geese 44
gendarmerie nationale 3
gendarmes 3, 92, 93
Geneva 9
German
    of Germany 91
Germany 30
Gladstone
    Betty 4, 11, 14, 35, 43, 57, 66, 67, 85, 103, 104, 105, 107, 108, 109, 110, 111, 112, 113, 114, 116, 117

Carol 2, 5, 6, 10, 11, 14, 16, 19, 23, 27, 35, 50, 51, 55, 59, 66, 67, 68, 71, 78, 79, 87, 91, 93, 96, 97, 103, 107, 111, 113, 116
Mr. 14, 15, 35
Roberta 2, 5, 6, 10, 11, 14, 16, 19, 23, 24, 27, 28, 35, 37, 50, 51, 55, 59, 62, 66, 67, 68, 71, 78, 87, 91, 93, 107, 111, 113
Gladstones
  reluctance admitting weakness 25, 26, 34, 86
  struggle to communicate 3, 12, 17, 20, 21, 23, 24, 77
goats 44, 54
Gorges of the Tarn
  guidebook 84
Goudet 24, 33
Goupil, Marius 14
Greece 2, 62
Greek
  of Greece 62
Grenoble 9
gun 15

H

hail 49, 50, 51
harness and saddle 4, 5, 7, 15, 16, 26
Harrison, John 17
hay 36, 37, 52, 54, 55, 59, 61, 93
heat 52, 54, 85, 87, 89, 91
Hellendorn
  Bernette 45
  family 44, 45, 47, 99, 100
  Nanette 44, 45, 47, 99
  Occo 45
  Rombout 41, 42, 43, 44, 45, 47, 99
Heritage Press 1
Holland 44, 45
horse 17
horseback 17, 63
hotel 5, 12, 14, 16, 19, 24, 29, 33, 39, 50, 51, 52, 55, 60, 62, 68, 69, 74, 77, 78, 79, 83, 87, 88, 89, 93, 95, 101, 111
hôtels
  La Bastide-Puylaurent 60
  Hôtel de la Gare, Chasseradès 68
  Hôtel de la Poste, Langogne 42
  Hôtel des Pins, La Bastide 61, 62, 65, 66, 108
  imaginary Logis de France 50, 51, 54, 55

I

Italy 6

J

Jaguar
  automobile 86
Jamon, Monsieur 5
Jeep 63
joke 36, 87

K

Kidnapped xi
kittens 93

L

L'Abbaye Notre Dame des Neiges 60
Landos 35
Langogne 40, 41, 48, 59, 99
laundry 47, 84
Les Alpiers 77
Loire River 24, 25
London xii, 4, 6, 105, 119
Long Walks in France xii
Le Luc-en-Provence 57, 58, 59, 63
  Our Lady statue 58
Lyon 106

M

le mairie (mayor's office) 13, 107, 111
map 1, 2, 5, 6, 12, 15, 40, 48, 49, 58, 69, 70, 71, 73, 76, 77, 80, 84
Mardi Gras 116

mayor
  of Bouchet 29
  of Goudet 24
  of Le Cheylard l'Evêque 51
  of Le Luc-en-Provence 59
  of Le Monastier-sur-Gazeille 3, 12, 13, 14, 16, 24, 29, 35, 107, 110, 111
  of St Jean du Gard 99
Mediterranean 81
  Sea 97
Mende 76
Michelin Tire Company 84
Mimente River 90, 91
Mirandol 70, 71, 74, 77
Modestine
  Gladstone's donkey 17, 18, 19, 20, 21, 22, 23, 24, 25, 26, 27, 28, 33, 34, 35, 36, 37, 38, 39, 40, 41, 42, 43, 45, 47, 48, 49, 50, 51, 52, 54, 58, 59, 61, 62, 65, 66, 67, 68, 69, 71, 74, 75, 77, 78, 79, 80, 81, 82, 83, 84, 85, 87, 89, 92, 95, 96, 97, 99, 100
  Stevenson's donkey 19, 35
monastery 17, 57, 60, 65, 67, 111
Le Monastier-sur-Gazeille xii, xiii, 2, 4, 5, 7, 11, 12, 13, 14, 15, 16, 17, 21, 22, 24, 25, 27, 35, 38, 60, 62, 82, 100, 101, 103, 104, 105, 106, 107, 110, 111, 112, 113, 116, 117
  church 17, 18, 19
Montagne de Goulet 69, 70, 73, 75, 76, 80, 81
Montagne de la Lozère 69, 73, 75, 76, 77, 78, 79, 81, 82, 90
Montagne Saint-Pierre 97
monument xii, 103, 104, 105, 106, 108, 109, 110, 111, 115, 117
motorbike 43, 44
motorcycles 17, 63
mountains
  Montagne de Goulet 69, 70, 73, 75, 76, 80, 81

  Montagne de la Lozère 69, 73, 75, 76, 77, 78, 79, 81, 82, 90
  Montagne du Goulet 69, 73, 75, 80
  Montagne Saint-Pierre 97
mouse 18
Mycenae 62

N

National Highway 37, 38, 40, 74, 76, 77, 84, 91
New England 17
New Orleans 116
newspaper xiii, 13, 22, 34, 53, 92, 105, 111, 116
newspapers 115
  La Montagne 34, 35
  Le Figaro 111
  New York Tribune 105
  San Francisco Chronicle 111
  The New York Times 105
  The Scotsman 111
New York 25, 119
Nicholson, Adam xii, 119
  Long Walks in France xii, 119
Nîmes 2

O

Olliers
  Doctor 14, 17, 35, 104, 105, 107, 108, 110, 113, 114
  Dominique 14, 116
  Madame 14, 15, 111, 114
  Pascal 14, 116
Olympia 62
Our Lady of the Snows 60, 108
Our Lady statue 58
oxen 60

P

packs 6, 19, 21, 26, 27, 36, 48, 52, 87, 88, 89, 95
packsaddle 10, 15, 16, 21
Pantal, Madame Alice 92, 97

Parayres
    Madame 38, 39
    Monsieur 38, 39
Paris 1, 36, 105, 111
passports 92, 93
people besides Gladstones who followed Stevenson's route
    Harrison, John 16, 17
    Singer, Vera 16, 62
    White, J. L. 16, 62
    Williamson, Shirley 16
    woman from New England 17
Père Émile 61, 62, 67, 68
Pic de Finiels 81
Place de la Poste 106
Place Saint-Jean 105, 106
plaque 105, 106, 107
plinth xii, 103, 104, 105
Pont-de-Barret 48
Le Pont-de-Montvert 76, 81, 82, 83, 84, 87, 89
post office 106, 117
Pradelles 35, 37, 38, 39, 40
Les Pradels 57, 58, 63
Protestant revolution 82
Le Puy-en-Velay 11, 16, 106, 107, 110

Q

The Questions 22, 77

R

rabbits 44
rain 6, 47, 48, 49, 50, 51, 57, 92, 93, 95
restrooms 30, 31, 47, 50, 54, 55, 92
Rhône River 11
rivers
    Allier River 40, 51, 58, 59, 68
    Le Chassezac River 74
    Gazeille River 11, 22
    Loire River 24, 25
    Mimente River 90, 91
    Rhône River 11
    Tarn River 82, 83, 84, 85, 90
RLS Society 105, 117

robbers 15
Robert, Madame Renèe 14, 15, 16, 17, 19, 38, 62, 77, 105, 106, 107, 113, 116
Robin, Monsieur 10, 15
Rome 62
Rouveirol
    Madame 14
    Monsieur and Madame 12
Royer, Monsieur 3, 4, 5, 13, 17, 20

S

Saint-Étienne 112
Sainte-Victoire 22
Saint Flour-de-Mercoire 50
Saint-Germain-de-Calberte 90, 92, 96, 97
Saint Jean-du-Gard 35, 63, 83, 97, 99, 101, 117
Saint-Jean, Madame 68, 69, 71, 74
Saint Laurent-de-la-Vernède 84, 85, 86
Saint-Martin-de-Fugères 22, 23
Salager, Maître 14
Sally, Mademoiselle 34
San Francisco 44, 45
San Francisco Chronicle 111
Santa Fe, New Mexico xii, 116
sausage 36, 53, 87, 89
Scotland 105
Senac
    Louis 25
    Monsieur 24, 25, 33
    Régis 25
sheep 54
sheets 30
short trousers 40
Singer, Vera 16, 62
slippers 90, 93
snow 45, 51, 75, 77, 78, 80, 81, 82
Spain 6, 30
stationmaster 68, 69, 70, 71
stèle 103
Stevenson, Alan 105

Stevenson, Robert Louis i, iii, v, xi, xii, xiii, 1, 2, 3, 5, 6, 11, 12, 14, 15, 16, 17, 18, 19, 24, 25, 26, 35, 40, 42, 48, 49, 57, 58, 59, 60, 62, 63, 69, 73, 74, 76, 77, 80, 81, 82, 84, 85, 89, 90, 97, 101, 103, 104, 105, 108, 110, 111, 116, 117, 119
    Kidnapped xi
    relatives
        Brackett, Nancy 105, 106, 108, 109, 111, 114
        Stevenson, Alan 105
    The Strange Case of Dr. Jekyll and Mr. Hyde xi
    Travels with a Donkey in the Cévennes xi, 1, 58, 77
    Treasure Island xi
stone pillars 79, 80, 81
The Strange Case of Dr. Jekyll and Mr. Hyde xi
swallows 81
Syndicat d'Initiative 13, 16, 20, 35, 99, 104, 105, 106, 107, 108, 111

T

Tarn River 82, 83, 84, 85, 90
tea 86, 97
telephone 27, 53, 60
television 104, 106, 109
Time-Life 105
Tiryns 62
toe deformity 85
toilet. *See* restrooms
Trappists 60, 68
Travels with a Donkey v, xi, 1, 11, 58, 77, 80, 86, 91, 110, 119
Travels with a Donkey in the Cévennes xi, 1, 58
Treasure Island xi

U

Les Uffernets 36, 37
United States xii, 9, 14, 15, 40, 55, 59
U. S. Geological Survey 1

V

Vaggiani
    Jean-Pierre 107, 108, 112, 113
    Monsieur Pierre 14
Valence 9, 11
Victory in Europe (VE) Day 24
Ville d'Ussel 26, 34
Villefort 76
Vin d'honneur 107, 111, 114
VW bus 91

W

weather
    cold 6, 30, 37, 40, 49, 51, 52, 53, 54, 56, 69, 78, 81, 89, 91
    gale 50
    hail 49, 50, 51
    heat 52, 54, 85, 87, 89, 91
    rain 6, 47, 48, 49, 50, 51, 57, 92, 93, 95
    snow 45, 51, 75, 77, 78, 80, 81, 82
    wind 50, 51, 81
White, J. L. 16, 62
Williamson, Shirley 16
wind 50, 51, 81
wine 11, 23, 50, 52, 68, 71, 97
wolves 15

Y

Yellow Submarine 113
youth hostel 6, 9, 38, 39, 40, 62

Z

zigzag 58, 77

About the Author

Betty Gladstone was born in 1919 in New York City. She earned a B. A. degree in psychology at the University of California at Berkeley. She and her first husband settled in Berkeley after graduation. While raising Roberta (born 1945) and Carol (born 1951), she administered health plan memberships for Kaiser and was active in the League of Women Voters. After 1965 she lived in France, then England, where she helped run a housing trust that rehabilitated old houses to create homes for low-income families. In 1979 she and her second husband returned to the United States for retirement in Santa Fe, New Mexico. She became an avid supporter of the Santa Fe Opera company, conducting back stage tours and soliciting local merchants for donations to fundraisers. Despite her lack of experience in retail, she was instrumental in opening a gift shop in the Opera complex to benefit the company. She died in Santa Fe in 1990.

Roberta Gladstone Croan had a varied career in engineering and industrial process development, working for Bechtel and Hewlett-Packard, among others. She retained her knack for languages, picking up conversational Czech, and, later on, Japanese. She was a gifted musician and dancer. Her daughter Deborah was born in 1973. Roberta died in Sacramento, California, in 2004. Her grandsons were born in 2008 and 2012.

Carol (now Carla) Gladstone worked in applied mathematics and scientific software at IBM and the MITRE Corporation before retiring in 2015. She is a hand weaver and volunteer at the Smithsonian's National Museum of Natural History. She lives in Bethesda, Maryland.

If You Liked this Book...

Would you be kind enough to leave a review for the book on Amazon, Goodreads, Barnes & Noble, iTunes, and other review sites? Thank you.

www.ingramcontent.com/pod-product-compliance
Lightning Source LLC
Chambersburg PA
CBHW050555300426
44112CB00013B/1933